Developing Your

Philosophy

of

Living

&

Leading

One Moment at a Time

D1506837

Maureen K. LeBoeuf
Brigadier General, U.S. Army, Retired

Former Master of the Sword
Department of Physical Education
United States Military Academy

Praise for *Developing Your Philosophy of Living and Leading One Moment at a Time*

"*Refreshingly pragmatic! General LeBoeuf teaches us about moments that matter. And that the key ingredients of humility, humor, resilience and matter of fact determination are critical in making the most of them.*"

Greg Brown
Chairman & CEO, Motorola Solutions

"*Maureen's book is a heartfelt story of building great leaders in a family of leaders. Maureen clearly shows that anchoring your leadership in core values built through a lifetime of learning and leading results in genuine leadership that people would follow to achieve high standards set for and by them. Maureen forces us all to realize that life is about tradeoffs as we build a career and life, we all need help and can reach our goals with focus and support. I know BG LeBoeuf well, and she has helped shape, build and change what has become a dynamic leadership culture at our company that has helped make us an industry leader. She helped make our entire company better and more effective leaders. This book will start you on your own journey of leadership discovery.*"

Tony Guzzi
Chairman, President, and CEO, EMCOR Group

"*Maureen's book is a beautiful mosaic of her life's lessons. She has brilliantly and transparently captured her journey, personal and professional, from childhood to General Officer, in relevant stories focused on daily self-leadership. Her vivid and relatable narrative will touch your heart and mind, have you laughing and crying, all while igniting a desire to make a greater positive impact on your own life and in the lives of others."*

Rebecca S. Halstead
Brigadier General, U. S. Army, Retired
CEO/Founder, Steadfast Leadership, LLC

"BG LeBoeuf is a gifted storyteller, and I found myself reflecting and asking questions about my own leader development journey with each page. This book is an enjoyable must-read, not a dry, clinical discussion of leadership. It will be valuable to all leaders, and those baby-boomers of Irish roots will certainly recognize and enjoy the great Keenan family upbringing and just may lose themselves in memories of their own past."

Frank Kearney
Lieutenant General, U.S Army, Retired

"By the age of 6 Maureen found herself a member of a 9-person squad and the middle child. Her position in the family provided her a unique view to observe each of us. Who knew she was watching so closely and taking notes? Mom and Dad would be quite proud to see so many family stories and lessons learned in print for a future generation of Keenans to read."

Leo E. "Timer" Keenan, III
Colonel, U.S. Army, Retired
Maureen's brother #1 of 9

"In a time of quick and easy communication, Maureen LeBoeuf reminds us of the art of storytelling. She tells stories from the heart that touch your mind and your heart. These 'moments that matter' are the very stories that teach us the complex life and leadership lessons we want and need. Maureen takes the stories to the reader with such authenticity and passion that you will remember them long after others. Readers will appreciate the journey from childhood to a career of

service and will find this book an important addition to their personal and professional library."

Glenn E. Pethel
Assistant Superintendent for Leadership Development
Gwinnett County Public Schools (GA)

"Like all great leaders, Brigadier General (ret) Dr. Maureen K. LeBoeuf leads by example. Sharing her personal stories, she reveals how the simple experiences of our lives provide the most profound lessons—if we are open to learning. I felt I became a better person after reading this book. LeBoeuf's wise words and rich stories revealed how the values I gained from my own life experiences can shape the actions I take to overcome adversity, achieve success and handle both with grace, integrity and dignity."

Dr. Paul Schempp
Professor, University of Georgia

"A must-read book for those building a meaningful career that integrates work and family! Maureen LeBoeuf has beautifully navigated a demanding career as a soldier, wife, mother, and educator. Her integration of passion, purpose, and values gives us a playbook for authentic leadership."

Sanyin Siang
CEO Coach and Executive Director
Duke University's Fuqua/Coach K Center
on Leadership & Ethics

Developing Your Philosophy of Living & Leading One Moment at a Time

ISBN: 9781092149501

DEDICATION

Dedicated To My Family

Ann F. Keenan and Leo E. Keenan, Jr.
My parents, who helped lay the foundation of strong values and stressed the importance of family and traditions and always reminded us to be proud to be Keenans. They were responsible for countless moments that mattered in my life.

Joe LeBoeuf
My husband, best friend, life partner and biggest cheerleader. I can't begin to thank you for walking side by side with me.
Because of you I work hard to be my best self, every day.

Jay and Jackie
I know this journey has not always been easy. I'm certainly glad that the two of you have been along for the ride. You are people of character, and for the I am proud.

And **Stephen**, I'm glad you are part of the family. I love you even though you went to the "other" academy.

Timer, Kathy, Judie, Bob, Dee Dee, Connie, Birdie and Kevin
My three brothers and five sisters, each of you has provided leadership, courage, laughter, drama, encouragement and a million big and little moments that have mattered in ways that you will never know.

TABLE OF CONTENTS

FOREWORD

At a time of unprecedented change and uncertainty in America, inspirational leadership has never been more important. Each of us is called upon daily to lead within our families, our professions and our communities. Are you ready to answer the call? Do you know what effective leadership looks like? Does one size fit all? How can you discover and develop your individual "true north" on your journey toward "Becoming Extraordinary" as a leader?

Brigadier General (US Army Retired) Maureen LeBoeuf has the answers and shares them with all of us in *Developing Your Philosophy of Living & Leading One Moment at a Time.* In this part memoir and part "how to" book, Maureen recounts compelling stories from her childhood, young adulthood and 28-year Army career, where she rose to senior rank at a time when women represented only one half of one percent of Army officers. Each story teaches an important universal lesson that all of us can learn and use in our daily lives.

I first met Maureen in 2010, when we were both tapped by President Obama to serve on the Defense Advisory Committee on Women in the Services (DACOWITS) — an independent body that advises the Secretary of Defense on issues affecting women in the military. Through DACOWITS, I first learned about Maureen's remarkable story and how she found her anchor in the uncertainty of life and leadership. From her beginnings, as one of 9 children in a traditional Irish Catholic family, to her college years at St. Bonaventure (school motto: Becoming Extraordinary); and through her 28-year Army career — from transportation officer, to helicopter pilot and culminating with her appointment as the first woman "Master of the Sword" (Director and Head of the Department of Physical Education at the prestigious US Military Academy at West Point) — Maureen describes the memorable people and experiences that shaped the leader she was to become. Her warmth, candor and easy-to-read style make the book truly enjoyable.

Best of all, Maureen then offers a practical, easy-to-follow approach on how you, too, can discover and develop your leadership philosophy and apply it at home and on the job.

Today, Maureen continues to lead — as a private leadership consultant and as Chair of the USO of North Carolina — and brings her universal leadership principles of vision, values, people development and change management to a variety of institutions and individuals. *Developing Your Philosophy of Living and Leading One Moment at a Time* is a book all aspiring leaders should read!

Deborah Lee James
23rd Secretary of the US Air Force
Author--*Aim High...Chart Your Course and Find Success*

AUTHOR'S NOTE

This book contains many stories based on my memories and times in my life, and they are written as such. I have changed the names of some individuals to protect their privacy.

ACKNOWLEDGEMENTS

Where does one begin to acknowledge and say thank you to the countless people who helped me on this journey? Quite simply, there are many people who need to be recognized for assisting me in the process of getting this book to print.

Thank you to my husband, Joe, who would patiently listen to my ideas for the book and give advice when asked.

Jay, Jackie and Stephen -- each of you has taught me a lot about leading, facing adversity, and following. I am most appreciative.

To each of my eight brothers and sisters, Timer, Kathy, Judie, Bob, Dee Dee, Connie, Birdie, and Kevin, for allowing me to share some of your stories. Growing up in a big family was challenging, interesting and mostly fun. Thank you!

A special thanks to my sister Birdie for reading the draft of this book at least four times. Having served as an English teacher for over thirty years, you provided advice, guidance, and an important critical eye.

To the soldiers with whom I had the privilege of serving, it was my great honor to do so. Each of you played a role in the soldier I became.

Thank you to the members of the United States Military Academy Corps of Cadets 1986-1988 and 1994-2004, whose lives in some way I had impacted. I couldn't be prouder to have played even a small role in your physical development and your having become leaders of character.

To the staff and faculty of the United States Military Academy Department of Physical Education, it was truly an honor to serve as an instructor, the Director of Instruction, and the Master of the Sword. Each time I served in DPE, I learned about Setting the Standard, Maintaining the Standard, and ultimately, Being the Standard!

To the Thayer Leader Development Group team, I am thankful that, at this point in my life, I found meaningful work. Yes, we make a difference!

To Susan Merlo and the Next Level iMedia team, thank you for helping me push this project across the finish line. Your professionalism, quick responses to my questions, and patience were appreciated more than you will ever know.

To my friends and colleagues who agreed to write endorsements for this book, I so appreciate your time and thoughtful comments. Thank you.

To the Honorable Deborah Lee James, who is such an amazing, talented woman, thank you for agreeing to write the foreword for this book.

Thank you to my Battle Buddies, Frank Kearney and Becky Halstead. I am fortunate beyond words to be able to work side-by-side with such incredible soldiers and leaders.

Finally, to all of you who, after hearing me speak, would ask the question, "When are you going to write a book?" Thank you for believing that my stories were worth putting into print where they just might have an impact.

INTRODUCTION

I was sitting in the foyer of Arvin Cadet Physical Development Center, home to the Department of Physical Education at the United States Military Academy (USMA) at West Point. In that opportune occasion of deep reflection, in the shadow of Carl Robert Arvin's[1] memorabilia, I realized it was time to tell my leadership story, a story built from many moments that have mattered throughout my life.

My journey to that particular moment began with a phone call in early February 1997 that came as a bit of a surprise. It was a call I had hoped to receive, but I was caught off guard when it came in as early as it did. I had applied for, and was interviewed to be, their next Director and Head of the Department of Physical Education. I did know that the discussion of the selection was going to the Academic Board[2] for a vote on that particular day in February, but because it is a position that must be approved by Congress, I was told that those who had applied would not know the results of the vote for quite some time.

---

[1] Carl Robert Arvin, member of USMA Class of 1965, captain of the 1964-65 wrestling team, and a three-year letter winner in wrestling. A captain in the infantry, he was killed in action in the Republic of Vietnam on 8 October 1967. He served as the Cadet Brigade Commander.

[2] The governing body of the Military Academy, members include the Superintendent, Dean, Commandant, Department Heads, Director of Admissions and the USMA Surgeon.

So, yes, I was surprised to hear the Commandant of Cadets' voice that day; he had chaired the search committee. As I answered the phone, I heard the familiar voice of the Commandant, "Maureen, this is General St. Onge."

He continued, "Maureen, I wanted to let you know that you have been selected to be the next Master of the Sword."[3] In that single moment, a thousand thoughts flew through my head. This was one of the few times in my life I was speechless. I thought about how my future would unfold. I knew that my philosophy of leadership and all of the lessons learned over the years leading up to that moment would provide the compass that would guide me as I readied myself for a plunge into a very uncertain world. I owed it to the folks in the department that I would now lead to arrive with a mindful, practical, and fully articulated statement of how I intended to behave, lead, and execute my stewardship responsibilities as the Department Head.

We all are called to lead in some way; it is a fundamental way we make a difference, have impact in our life, in the lives of others, and in the world. This leadership happens in many ways: in our own families and communities, as the heads of major organizations, or through our ability to effectively navigate our individual lives in a very complex world. We cannot escape the requirement to have clarity on how we live and lead or to understand the internal, values-driven compass that controls how we navigate in the world.

This book is about how my compass came to be. It is about the many moments that mattered in my life: those that built my compass, enabled my view on living and leading, and the fundamental

---

[3] The Master of the Sword (MOS) is the historic title given to the Director and Head of the Department of Physical Education at West Point. In 1816 Thomas Pierre was selected to teach physical education at the United States Military Academy. He was the first full-time physical educator in higher education in the country. He taught fencing and was a Sword Master.

principles of leadership that are my true north and have served as my anchor in the uncertainty that is life and leadership.

I begin this book where my leadership lessons first began, with my family. I grew up in a large family, the middle child of nine. Being a member of such a big group one learns a lot, and I learned from each one of my siblings. Communication was one of the biggest takeaways from being in a big family. My eight brothers and sisters are all very different people, and at a young age I had to figure out how to communicate with each one.

After acquainting you with my siblings and the lessons I learned from each of them, in the next part of this book will take you further through my life's journey as I share stories about some very significant moments in my life. Interestingly, some of the stories will at first sound small or trivial, like my sister bringing home a second-place ribbon she won in a swimming event, or a visit from the Mother Superior to my fourth-grade class, or even my experience as a high school varsity cheerleader. (Yes, I was a cheerleader!) And, some of these stories will sound rather far-fetched today, like when I entered the Army as a second lieutenant and was told I would never attend the Army's flight program, or even more interesting, when I was told I would never ever teach in the Department of Physical Education at the United States Military Academy. As you'll see as each of my stories unfold, however, the moments I write about, both great and small, were all profound and truly altered the trajectory of my life, bringing me to that point in time when I was sitting in the foyer of Arvin Cadet Physical Development Center, deciding to write this book.

These are my stories. Come along for the ride and see the kinds and types of experiences that have shaped me as a leader.

CHAPTER ONE

GROWING UP KEENAN

THE FAMILY

I am the middle child of nine children – yes nine – from one of those big, Irish, Catholic families. The age range amongst my siblings and me is eleven years, made up of six girls and three boys – nine single births in eleven years. And, yes, my mom is a 'saint.' I'm the third girl – the middle girl – and born on my brother Bobby's first birthday. My fighting for a place in this world began early with a shared birthday, and it carried through well into my childhood.

For example, my two older sisters are named Kathy and Judie, and so it was common for Dad to say, when addressing me, "Kathy, Judie, what's your name?" I would respond because I knew whom he was addressing. However, one would think he would call me Mo, my very easy to remember nickname – it's only two letters. How hard was that to remember? It rhymes with no! There were times I would say to my parents, tongue in cheek, "I'm number five in line but number nine in your hearts" or, "I'm overlooked and under-loved." Mom would respond, "Oh Maureen!" She never once disagreed with me, though – never once!

Because you can't follow the players in my story without a program, let me give you the lineup of the siblings:

#1   Leo E. Keenan, III – nickname: Timer[4]

#2   Kathleen – nickname: Kathy

#3   Judith – nickname: Judie[5]

#4   Robert – nickname: Bobby or Speedy[6]

#5   Maureen – nickname: "Mo" (Mo Mo when I was younger)[7]

#6   Deirdre – nickname: Dee Dee

#7   Constance – nickname: Connie (also called Roger for a brief period after a nap-time haircut from Dee Dee)

#8   Eileen – nickname: Birdie (she used to run through the house flapping her arms like a bird)

#9   Kevin – nickname: Butchie (I believe this was the result of a butch haircut)

I vividly remember the night I became the middle child of nine. It was July 8, 1960, and Dad came into our bedroom and said, "There is a full moon tonight, and you have a new baby brother. His name is Kevin."

---

[4] Mom agreed to name her first-born son Leo, however did not want to call him Leo. Apparently, he was born on time, thus the name. I never gave this nickname any thought until high school when someone asked, "What kind of name is Timer?"

[5] Judie changed how she spelled her name from Judy to Judie; I thought that was so cool!

[6] Bob was the smallest guy on the high school football team. He ran fast to get away from the others.

[7] I started placing quotations around my name ("Mo") in an attempt to have a cool name like Judie.

We were living at 133 North Barry Street in Olean, New York. It was too small a place to live with so many children, but honestly I don't ever remember it being crowded. I slept in a bedroom with two sets of bunk beds and learned how to co-habituate a very small space with three other sisters – Dee Dee, Connie, and Birdie.

Our dad, Leo, often referred to as Keek, was a college professor at St. Bonaventure University, also in Olean. Dad spent fifty-two years on the faculty at St. Bonaventure University (often referred to fondly as Bonas), an iconic figure in the history of the university for sure. He earned his undergraduate degree at Bonas, master's degree at Cornell, and received an honorary doctorate from Bonas later in his tenure. Our mother was highly educated as well, earning her master's degree in chemistry by age 20. She was, in a word, brilliant. She was the second child born to Robert and Anna Finlay. Anna was a nurse, and Bob owned his own plumbing business. Anna knew that mom was smart and always insisted that she be put at the front of the classroom. No alphabetical seating for Ann Finlay! Mom excelled in school and actually skipped a few grades.

When I was a junior in college and turned twenty-two, Mom said to me, "When I was your age, I had a master's degree in chemistry, was married and had a child."

My response? "Well Mom, I guess I'm an underachiever."

From these highly educated roots, all nine of us Keenans are Bonas grads, and seven Keenan family grandchildren are SBU graduates as well. We are a legacy family, true citizens of St. Bonaventure and its Catholic community, with deep roots in Olean. I loved Bonaventure then and still do. It was my home away from home and a significant influence on the person I am and what I stand for.

I have to admit, I was not a great academic student when I was young, especially when it came to math and some of the sciences. Mom was a math savant, really; and it was frustrating for her to have a child who didn't seem to get math. It was almost as if I had the math gene and was stubbornly refusing to use it. The dining room table in our home became the proverbial torture chamber for math instruction, and for me, crying was most often the outcome.

Academically, as a group, my siblings and I were all over the place. Several of my brothers and sisters are very bright, on the honor roll and members of the National Honor Society. Judie, who is a few years older than I am, always did extremely well in school. When we would be out back playing kickball, Judie would be in the house studying. One time as I approached home base, which was a very large bare spot, I looked up and saw Judie in the bathroom window looking out. I remember thinking that I was glad I was outside playing ball, and not 'stuck' in the house. Her absence, however, did make the teams even, four on each side which worked out well for all since she was happiest being inside, reading and studying.

THE BOYS

My brothers, two of whom anchored the sibling lineup of our team, the oldest and the youngest, played a significant role in the family story and in my moments. Here is a bit about each and some of the lessons I've learned from having them in my life.

TIMER

Leo E. Keenan, III (Timer) – Timer is the oldest, the first born. I can't begin to imagine what it was like to be the oldest of nine children – the first to do everything, the first one parented. I found that being in a big family and separated by several years made it easy to have a better relationship with Timer. He is four years older than I, and we simply seemed to click, possibly because there are three siblings between us and because he was a boy. We have always gotten along well and share a special connection.

To me, Timer was the epitome of a big brother. He was an athlete, popular, cool (at least I thought so) and, most importantly, he was always nice to me. Timer had a paper route with the *The Olean Times Herald*, and some of our siblings begrudgingly helped him with his route. I liked helping because it enabled me to spend time with him. The papers were dropped off, the number seventy-seven written in grease pencil on a blank sheet wrapped around the papers. Timer would cut the string, and prior to setting out on his multi-block route, he would distribute the papers to those of us who helped. One to the police station, two to the City Club and so on. Of course, he carried the bulk of the papers, but we helped. The Palace movie theater and Fanny Farmer candy store were both on his route, so sometimes he would stop and get candy. I remember him coming home with some M&Ms and giving me some. It was a real treat. He didn't share with everyone, only me; these were significant moments that made me feel special.

We all attended St. Mary of the Angels School in Olean. During the 8th grade there was a traditional class trip. It was an opportunity to go someplace away from Olean – someplace cool! Timer's class went to Crystal Beach, an amusement park located near Buffalo. Going that far away then was like taking a weekend trip to London today. The day of his class trip, we were all in the backyard playing when he returned home from this significant adventure. He walked through an alley from Main Street that led to our house and up to the backyard fence. He was wearing a sailor cap with a large button that read, *Kiss Me I'm Irish!* To us kids, Timer was the best, and so I thought this was the neatest thing ever. I even wondered if any of the eighth-grade girls had kissed him, not only because he was Irish, but because he was Timer – the King of Cool!

On one of my birthdays after the presents had been opened, Timer jumped up and said to me, "I have a gift for you!" He ran upstairs and came back down with a black, velvet box. I opened it slowly and inside was a stretchy (elastic) diamond bracelet. Of course, it was something he had won at a carnival, or maybe he won it during his trip to Crystal Beach. Nonetheless, it was mine, and it was special because it was from Timer. I loved my bracelet! It was not the only piece of jewelry I received from Timer. In high school he was dating a girl and they broke up. She mailed back black onyx earrings and a matching bracelet. Timer gave them to me.

I listened to Timer. Once in high school I asked him what he thought Dad would do if I drank. He said, "You don't need to worry about Dad; you need to worry about me!" Girls who have older sisters most likely look up to them, and I have two older sisters, but it was Timer whom I admired. I didn't drink my first beer until I was nineteen-and-a-half; the drinking age at the time in New York was eighteen.

Being a member of a big family presents many opportunities, moments that matter, to learn simply by observing the actions and behavior of the others. You have to be willing to pay attention.

Once Timer was left in charge when Mom and Dad went out for the evening. We had a big backyard and would spend hours playing out back. Kickball was the game of choice. However, on one occasion Timer began hitting golf balls in the backyard, not heeding Dad's directive not to hit golf balls there. One ball, a finely stuck nine-iron, went flying over the fence and through a glass windowpane of a neighbor. I remember how we all looked, standing there with our mouths open. Oh my gosh, Timer broke a window, and only bad can follow, or so we thought.

Without hesitation, Timer hopped over the fence, walked across the parking lot, and knocked on the door. He told our neighbors that he had hit the golf ball. Of course, when Mom and Dad came home Timer told them what had happened, and the windowpane was repaired. For his birthday, Dad gave Timer the repair bill for the window – framed. At the bottom was typed, *Dad was right, again!*

I'm sure the neighbors could have figured out who hit the golf ball. However, as a little girl I was impressed that Timer had the courage to tell our neighbors and take responsibility for his behavior. I learned the power of accountability and the respect that being accountable engenders. Timer was our sibling model of a person of character.

We had a very specific route that we were required to take to and from elementary school – mapped out for safety and accountability, for sure. Out the front door on Barry Street, take a right and cross State Street, and continue to Henley Street where we would take a right; continue to Union Street, and a few hundred yards ahead on the left was our school. Dad always said that the reason we all took the same route was in case there was ever an emergency during the time we were walking to and from school, he could drive the route from Barry Street to Henley Street and pick us all up.

One particular morning there was quite a snowstorm; frankly, it was blizzard-like and typical for Western New York. Later that morning the phone rang. It was the photographer for the Olean Times Herald, our local newspaper. He told mom that he took a picture of Timer crossing Union Street in front of the Olean House. The photographer knew Timer was a Keenan, and he wanted to make sure he had Timer's first name correct for the caption. Mom gave him the information and hung up.

Later that evening with the Olean Times Herald paper in hand, Dad asked Timer what route he had taken to school that morning. Of course, he responded with the required script, up Barry Street to Henley Street. Then Dad (with a characteristic level of flair in these type of moments) opened the paper to the page with Timer's picture. In spite of the falling snow, it was a great picture, clearly Timer. He was busted.

Apparently, while Timer delivered the paper, he evidently didn't read the paper. Otherwise, he would have known the jig was up and surely would have had an explanation handy. Also, in my nine years attending St. Mary's, not once did Mom or Dad, because of an emergency, ever pick me up!

Moments that mattered with Timer taught me the following:

- Be accountable. Take responsibility for my behavior, even when it is hard.
- Do the right thing at the right time for the right reason.
- Character matters!

BOBBY

Bobby is #4, and he and I share a birthday, December 7th. I recall one year we were going to have a big birthday party. The morning of our birthday I awoke early, and Bobby was covered with red spots. I said, "Bobby, what have you been doing?" Let's just say it wouldn't have been unusual for him to be into Mom's lipstick or fooling around with a magic marker.

He said, "Nothing!" I marched him into the bathroom to look at his face. Next stop, Mom and Dad's bedroom.

"Mommy, look at Bobby!" Although she was asleep, the excitement in my voice startled her.

Mom woke up, took one look at Bobby and said, "It's the chicken pox."

Needless to say, there was no birthday party. Within a week or so, the rest of us had the chicken pox, all thanks to Bobby! The living room looked like an infirmary with Mom going from one child to the next applying pink calamine lotion with cotton balls. Of course, we were told not to scratch. Later in December of that year, only one child was in the picture with our grandfather, Poppy, and Dad cutting down the Christmas tree – Bobby.

Bobby was a fairly good athlete. He swam and played golf and football. When we were in high school, he started experiencing a lot of pain – all over his body. I vividly remember hearing him at night crying because of it. At sixteen years of age he was diagnosed with rheumatoid arthritis. One day I saw him walking next to our grandfather who was in his 80s at the time. Their gaits, the way they walked, were strikingly similar. Bobby walked like an old man. He has lived with this pain for almost his entire life, and he has never complained. Once, when I asked him if he hurts often, he said matter-of-factly, "I'm in pain constantly."

I can't imagine being in pain constantly. There are times when I have a pain, and I think about Bobby. I know I can take some pain medication and my pain will go away. His pain is a constant companion.

What is truly interesting about Bob is that he has a wonderful sense of humor. He has a quick wit and can tell a joke. He has written e-mails telling stories that honestly will have me laughing out loud. In one such e-mail, he wrote about taking some cookies from Mom and Dad's house. However, these were no ordinary cookies, not chocolate chip or oatmeal; these were Mom's legendary spritz cookies. These cookies were purported to even have healing qualities. Try as we might, no one has ever made a spritz cookie quite like Mom. The fact that they were only made around the holidays made them even more precious. Here is a portion of the e- mail Bob sent to us.

"...I popped the cover off my ill-gotten goods and I stared at it as I rounded the corner and turned onto Clinton Street. WOW I can't believe it...here on the seat before me is the Rosetta Stone, the Holy Grail, the Fountain of Youth...all mine...what is this on the top? A label and a number...I pulled over under the illumination of a dim streetlight to read the text...

TO: Kevin

FROM: Mom

Batch #1741

Should I continue around the block with Batch #1741 ... NAW...Homeward bound a plain baloney sandwich in one hand and a SPRITZ COOKIE WITH CHOCOLATE SPRIN- KLES IN THE OTHER!!! Life just doesn't get any better than this...Sorry Kevin...

Sign me the Outlaw

PS to Timer...If you think 3 spritz cookies cured/healed your ailment while in Buffalo, you should see what a whole boxful (60-75) can do for you."

Moments that mattered with Bobby taught me the following:

- Demonstrate grace in the adversity of suffering.
- With regard to complaining, remember there is always some-one worse off or in more pain.
- A good sense of humor matters.

KEVIN

Kevin, or 'Butch' as he is more affectionately known, is #9 of nine, the youngest, the baby, the favorite – you get the picture! Actually, Kevin is a great guy, and we have always had a special relationship. I'm not sure how that happens in a big family, but it does.

Kevin was an interesting little boy, observant and with an in-credible and active imagination. He would sit in the bay window in our house on Barry Street and watch the cars. I was amazed with his accumulated knowledge of cars; he knew all the makes and models. To this day, I wonder why he is not the owner of a car dealership.

Like most little boys, Kevin was fascinated with super heroes. One day as I walked through the living room, he was there with a piece of string tied around each wrist and the other end taped to the wall. Of course, he was Spider-Man, and with his own sound effects he was dispensing his web. I recall thinking, *Well this is interesting, but at least he won't get into trouble.* He had and would wear the costumes of Super Man, Spider-Man, and a Royal Canadian Mounted Policeman. There is a picture of Kevin as a Royal Canadian Mounted Policeman in the full regalia of the red serge (the jacket) with the cross-strap and belt, blue pants with a yellow stripe and, of course, the felt ranger hat. He looked fabulous and always took himself very seriously when he was 'in uniform.'

As a result of his imagination he had a couple of 'friends' who lived in his ears. Yes, Charlie Hadlie and Rat Fink were Kevin's imaginary friends. Periodically he would talk about them.

Dad had a ukulele, which we were not allowed to touch. On occasion we would sit and listen to Dad play various songs. *Jimmy Cracked Corn* was a favorite. Yes, I touched, and even worse, played the ukulele when Dad was out of the house and Mom was not within earshot. In fact, I think it's safe to say that most of us played with the ukulele at one time or other.

One evening Dad gathered us in the living room for a talk. He pulled out his ukulele; the strings were broken.

Dad said, "Someone in this room broke the strings on my ukulele." He went on to say, "I would appreciate it if that person would speak up." We sat there in silence for a period of time that seemed to go on forever. I thought about how I had played Dad's ukulele, but I didn't break it.

Kevin raised his hand and said, "I didn't break it, but I know who did."

I thought, *Oh my gosh, he is going to tattle on someone! What if he says I did it?* Of course I didn't do it; but if Kevin said I did, would Dad believe him?

Dad looked at Kevin and said, "So Kevin, who broke my ukulele?" Without missing a beat and very seriously Kevin said, "Rat Fink." You could feel the tension lift in the room as the rest of us shared a collective sigh of relief.

Dad, holding back a smile, said, "How do you know Rat Fink broke the ukulele?"

Kevin said, "I was there."

So, there you have it. Rat Fink had done the deed. Kevin was a witness. It was interesting that he fessed up but not quite. As a little boy he knew he needed to let Dad know who broke the ukulele but didn't want to admit he did it; thus, he blamed his imaginary friend.

Over the years Kevin would continue to talk about Charlie Hadlie and Rat Fink. However, they were never again blamed for something he had done. Kevin figured out at that young age that you don't throw your buddies under the bus.

I have learned a lot from Kevin about leading and following. Leaders need to have people around them who think differently and have imaginations. These are people who can help the leader imagine what is possible. Leaders need to create an environment in which people know they can give the boss the bad news. I have a colleague who says, "Walk to me with good news; run to me with bad news."

Moments that mattered with Kevin taught me the following:

- It's important to have an imagination, and sometimes it's okay to remember what it was like to be a little kid.

- Being accountable matters and cannot be outsourced to a Charlie Hadlie or Rat Fink. It cannot be externalized; it has to owned.
- Bad news matters; humility allows leaders to hear it.

THE GIRLS

Dad was strict – Irish Catholic strict. He had certain rules that were established that especially impacted the girls. I'm not sure how he came up with his rules, but he had them. It was the 50s and 60s when we were growing up. It was a different time. There were no nylon stockings until 8th grade graduation and no makeup until freshman year in high school. I'm sure there was a no dating rule as well. When Judie and Kathy went to high school dances, Dad would pick them up immediately after the dance. There was no lollygagging and no giggling as they walked along with girlfriends talking about the boys they had danced with. They went directly to the waiting car. Frankly, I don't recall any similar rules applied to the behavior of the boys.

KATHY

The second child in line is Kathy, the oldest girl, who had to effectively plow the ground of family life for the girls that followed. She is three years older than I. Kathy was enough older that I would constantly watch her, how she behaved, and the outcomes of her behavior, particularly against Dad's stated and emerging rules. There were plenty of times when I was glad that I was not the oldest girl in the rules-navigational challenge.

One of the rules was that we were not allowed to get our ears pierced. However, Kathy, like most teenage girls, wanted to get her ears pierced, so one day, with the help of a friend armed with ice cubes and a sterilized needle, she did exactly that. Her friend threaded a needle and pulled a piece of thread through her ear lobes. In order to cover the newly pierced ears Kathy was wearing a bandana, however one ear wasn't quite covered and the thread in the hole showed. Mom noticed and said, "The next thing you are going to do is run away and get married!" At the time, Kathy was 14 and didn't even have a boyfriend. The decision was made that Kathy could keep her ears pierced. In fact, Mom took Kathy to a local jewelry store and purchased a good quality pair of earrings so Kathy's ears wouldn't get infected.

We were also not allowed to wear two-piece bathing suits. Again, Kathy, striving to fit in with the other teenage girls, purchased a two-piece. It was pink with a white overlay that connected to the top of the suit. The overlay covered her stomach. The suit was quite modest. However, once the suit was discovered it was put in Mom's cedar chest. You have to give Kathy credit for trying.

On Easter we wore sister dresses, and all six girls would line up for the annual picture wearing identical dresses. Each year we would look over Mom's shoulder as she would thumb through the Spiegel mail-order catalog and select the same dress in six different sizes. For me, this was thrilling. Looking at the catalog, filling out the order form, putting the order in the mail and waiting for the package to arrive. You can only imagine the excitement when the mailman would deliver the box. It was opened, sizes were checked, and Easter dresses were handed out. We would run to our rooms, quickly changing out of our play clothes to try them on.

One year the dresses were bright pink with large white daisies with a yellow center. Kathy was a junior in high school. I wondered if she was embarrassed wearing the same dress as her five younger sisters, the youngest being eight years old, or was simply used to this being one of the rules of life as the oldest girl in a large family.

When you are a girl and have an older sister or sisters, you learn a lot by simply watching. You learn how to wear makeup, what clothes to wear and when, how to talk to boys on the phone, and how to navigate the difficult world of dating. Unfortunately, I never learned any of this from Kathy. No doubt Dad's rules hindered this aspect of Kathy's experiences as a teenager.

One day after swim team practice at the YMCA, I stood mesmerized as I watched two of the older girls put on mascara. I asked, "What grade are you in?"

One of them replied, "We are in seventh grade."

I was shocked they were younger than Kathy and wearing make-up. I wondered how they learned to do this; who taught them? To me they seemed so much older.

I started my high school career at Archbishop Walsh High School. When the academic year started so did the school dances. I love to dance, and so I enjoyed them. The first few dances, Dad would be outside the school waiting, and I thought, *I can't do this. Not fun!* So, one evening before a dance, I took a chance and asked Dad if I could walk home from the dance when it ended. I told him I would not stop and come right home. And, to my surprise, he said yes. I took another chance a few weeks later when I asked if I could stop at the soda shop near Walsh where all the kids hung out after dances. He again said yes, however I was to get a soda, drink it and head home, no hanging out. With each approval, I made sure that I did as I was asked, knowing that if I gained Dad's trust, he might allow me some additional privileges later in high school.

I was not always perfect, and on occasion I was late. Being late in our house was the worst. Dad never went to bed until all his children were home and accounted for. And there was no sneaking into the house, no sir. Dad sat in 'his chair' in the living room enabling an unobstructed view of the comings and goings into our home. There was a window perpendicular to the front door and as you approached the entrance to the house, you could barely see Dad's leg. It was not a big deal unless you were late, and he was sitting in his bathrobe. That was a visible indication that he was ready for bed but had to stay up. The bathrobe was brown, white and yellow seersucker with a brown belt. It is legendary in our family, and a memory that is both wonderful and terrible, all at the same time. We all have our own, *Dad sitting in his bathrobe as we came in late* story. Of course, some stories are better than others.

Many years later, while stationed in Colorado at Fort Carson for two years, my family and I lived across the street from Timer and his family. One evening Timer called and asked me to come over. I walked in and there he was sitting in his chair and wearing Dad's bathrobe. Apparently, Dad had sent it to him. With Timer being the oldest and having the oldest children, I suppose Dad thought it was time to pass the baton, or rather, the bathrobe. When I saw him sitting there, I had a visceral response, an elevated heart rate coupled with a gasp as my memories of Dad and his robe crashed over me like a big wave at the beach. I didn't disappoint Timer. He got exactly the reaction from me that he expected.

I continued to get additional privileges in high school, and during my sophomore year, I began dating. The boys in Olean knew of my dad, and it was always interesting the first time a boy came to the house to pick me up for a dance or the movies.

I would tell them, "Just look my Dad in the eye and give him a firm handshake." I never thought that any of them were very comfortable around Dad, and of course he liked it that way.

After high school I went to St. Bonaventure University for college. Another one of Dad's rules was that none of his daughters would live on campus. Timer lived on campus his freshman year. Near the end of my second semester sophomore year, I decided I wanted to live on campus. After all, I spent hours on campus each day. I attended class, went to swim team practice, worked at the pool and had a boyfriend. I wondered how I could get Dad to agree to allow me to live on campus. I knew that a face-to-face would not work because as soon as I would ask the question, he would have immediately said no.

So, I wrote Dad a letter. My thinking was that he would get the letter, read it and then he would ruminate over my request. In the letter I made the argument that I was already spending so much time on campus that valuable study time was wasted commuting back and forth between home and Bonaventure. I wrote the letter and mailed it to Dad's post office box, which happened to be Box #1 at the St. Bonaventure post office. Obviously, it took only a day for the letter to arrive in Dad's on-campus mailbox. I actually went into the post office two days in a row to check on it. The first time I saw the letter sitting in Dad's box, the second day it was gone.

I knew he must have read it. He checked his post office box each day, which was part of his daily ritual around campus. I felt a bit awkward around Dad for the next few weeks, knowing he had received and read the letter, yet he didn't acknowledge receipt let alone that it was read. One day I was going to catch a ride home with Dad after my day of classes and swim team practice had concluded.

I got in the car and Dad said, "I received your letter."

I sat there and thought, *Well, here we go.*

He continued, "Your mother and I have talked, and we have agreed that you can live on campus."

To my surprise, my strategy worked! I knocked down another barrier, since Kathy and Judie never lived on campus. I was the first girl in the family to do so and set the conditions for those who followed me. My three younger sisters, Dee Dee, Connie and Birdie all were able to live on campus during their college years. Thank you very much.

Moments that mattered with Kathy taught me the following:

- Because of Kathy I found my voice, and for that I am eternally grateful. I learned to speak up and ask for what I want. After all, when you ask, the worst that can happen is that the response is no. However, when the answer is yes, good outcomes can result, and not just for oneself. Dee Dee, Connie and Birdie all benefitted from Dad saying yes to me because all three were allowed to live on campus.

JUDIE

Judie is the third child, second girl. Mom would often say that after three children there never seemed to be an increase in the commotion in the family; and it appeared this reasoning made it easier to have more kids. I suppose once there were three, our parents had to go into a zone defense.

Judie is smart, a veracious reader, took piano lessons and was a huge help around the house to Mom. It probably didn't hurt that she liked the house to be nice and neat, which was a real challenge in a house with nine children. It also made her a natural as Mom's prized assistant.

Judie was three years ahead of me in school. She would learn something new at school and come home and teach me. We had a wonderful, old classroom chalkboard that was mounted on a wall in the house. It had a sill at the bottom where broken pieces of chalk and an eraser were held. I learned how to diagram compound sentences in first grade thanks to Judie. Of course, I had to wait three years to utilize that skill.

I actually remember some of the projects Judie did in school because to me they were so impressive. For example, Judie did a project in 7th grade on the Intercontinental Ballistic Missile. The title of her report was, "Ready, Fire, Aim." To prepare, Judie wrote to an uncle, a United States Air Force officer, for assistance, and he sent her pictures. For the cover she even made a rocket out of cardboard and wrapped it in aluminum foil, and she drew flames of fire coming out of the bottom of the rocket. Attention to detail was her watchword. I was amazed at this project, the time she worked on it, and especially the cover. Of course, she got an A.

Another paper Judie wrote was about the continent of Africa. She painstakingly cut out several pages of lined paper in the shape of the continent of Africa, and then she carefully wrote her report on those pages. Again, I was amazed, impressed and inspired. I learned the importance of attention to detail in schoolwork, and the power of giving the best possible effort under all conditions.

There must have been a certain grade in which there was a requirement to write about a continent because when that time came for me, I wrote about Australia. I decided I would trace the outline of Australia on each sheet of paper, so it was somewhat of a watermark on my paper. Cutting out each page as Judie had done was no doubt a bit more work that I was willing to do. Proud of my work, I handed in my paper, and I'm not sure exactly when I discovered this, but I had traced Australia upside down on every page. Panic set in when I realized there was nothing I could do. Fortunately for me the teacher didn't notice. I don't recall the grade, but I learned a significant lesson around double-checking my work.

Once Judie was old enough, she would watch us when Mom and Dad went out for the evening. After they departed, Judie would assign each of us a cleaning task. This involved a lot of work – dusting, vacuuming, and picking up. When our jobs were completed, we would have singing practice. Judie would line us up around the baby grand piano, and we would sing. She was a tough task-master. We had to sing the songs according to her arrangement. On one occasion, and I suspect there were many, I was fooling around. Judie got quite angry and shoved me against the wall. Not only did it scare me, but it knocked the wind out of me, and I slid down to the floor. I saw the look of fear in Judie's eyes – she thought she had hurt me. So, I stayed on the floor a bit longer than necessary, milking the situation for all it was worth. That was the last time I recall ever fooling around during singing practice with Judie in charge.

For one of our singing intros, we would crouch down behind the piano and pop-up and sing our name. Sung to the tune, "Whistle While You Work" from the Disney movie *Snow White*, we would sing "Mo Mo, and Dee Dee, Connie and Birdie." I liked those re-hearsals and especially the performances.

Dad would purchase LP albums – *The Sound of Music, Mary Poppins, Camelot*, and countless others. We would learn the songs and perform for Lala and Poppy, our grandparents. Our performances of course provided another opportunity to wear our sister dresses, although Kathy never sang with us.

Growing up, Judie and I were especially close. I believe because Judie is a few years older and we didn't share a bedroom, it was easier to get along. I looked up to Judie even though she stopped growing in 4th grade. She topped off at 5' even, and I at 5'9". As mentioned earlier, I loved the school projects she did and tried hard to emulate her performance.

Judie has a gentle spirit and always seemed to be an old soul. She is one of the most thoughtful and kind individuals I know. I'm not sure Judie has ever been mean to anyone. From an early age, Judie recognized the importance of a hand-written note. One time I was going on a trip, and she gave me a handmade card. It had illustrations of Winnie the Pooh and her, and she wrote a sweet note. I'm sure I cried when I read the card.

Moments that mattered with Judie taught me the following:

- I learned about working hard. In everything she did, Judie went the extra mile (or two) and her hard work always made a difference.
- I learned about excellence. As a smart girl, Judie didn't have to put so much thought and creativity into her school projects – she would have gotten great marks anyway. But doing her best was always important to Judie and her drive to set the bar high for herself inspired me to strive toward excellence as well.
- I learned about being kind and how a person can be kind without being weak – an outstanding attribute for a leader.

DEE DEE

Dee Dee is the sixth child, the fourth girl and seventeen months younger than I. This is also a fact that is often mentioned in family gatherings. As a little girl, Dee Dee could be rather loud and fresh. In fact, Dad often referred to her as the freshest kid on the block. I recall Dad calling Dee Dee over to him and then pretending that there was a volume button on her tummy, which he would turn down. In high school I would often embarrass Dee Dee because she didn't like me speaking to her in the hallway.

So, I would yell, "Hi, Dee Dee!"

Of course, her response was a roll of the eyes, and I'm sure if I had been close enough, I would have also heard a click of her tongue.

In a big family there are squabbles, and Dee Dee and I had our share growing up. We were close in age, and we shared a bedroom. One Christmas we were getting the lights and ornaments out, and I accidentally broke an ornament.

Dee Dee yelled, "Mo broke an ornament!"

21

Thanks, Dee Dee, I thought, *Great, now I'm going to get in trouble.*

From the other room Mom responded, "Clean it up, I'm sure it was an accident."

I was dating a boy who once wrote me a note that Dee Dee found and proceeded to hand over to Dad. I have no idea the contents of that note, but I do remember the lecture I received from Dad.

Thanks again, Dee Dee!

There were times when we were all together and Dad would say, "Look around the room, look at your brothers and sisters. Someday they will be your best friends."

Yeah, right, I remember thinking, *this will never happen.*

When Dee Dee and I were in college and living at home, we began a weekly ritual. After classes on Friday, we would stop at the grocery store and purchase a loaf of soft Italian bread, potato chips, Mountain Dew™, and Hostess™ cupcakes. We would go home and make scrambled egg sandwiches that we would eat with the chips, then eat the cupcakes and drink the Dew as we watched the soap opera, *All My Children*. A great memory of sisterhood.

Dad was right, again. Over the years Dee Dee and I have become very good friends. She went into the Army after graduation from St. Bonaventure and asked me to administer her oath of office. It was a wonderful honor. And, I'm the godmother to her daughter, Katie – an even bigger honor.

Moments that mattered with Dee Dee taught me the following:

- People change and grow. It's important to put 'stuff' behind you. Adhering to the expression, look forward and glance back, has helped me tremendously as a leader. I have forgiven Dee Dee for giving Dad the note from my high school boyfriend, I think.

CONNIE

Push, push, push. When I think of Connie growing up, that is how I think of her. She constantly pushed the envelope, pushed the limits, and always pushed back on the rules. I'm sure in another family, Connie's behavior would have been no big deal. In our family, eight of us did as we were asked. Not so for Connie. She challenged Mom and Dad a lot. Often, it seemed a matter of sport.

Dad would use the familiar expression, "If I ask you to jump, I want you to ask how high on the way up."

While we would be in the air, Connie would remain sitting and say, "Why are we jumping?"

Connie is a night owl, and as a kid she did not like getting up for school until she absolutely had to. We would all be up, dressed and eating breakfast, and mom would send us upstairs at various intervals to wake up Connie. It was so irritating. I thought mom should let her oversleep and deal with the wrath of the nuns.

Earlier, I mentioned dad sitting up late in his chair, waiting for one or more of his children to come home. Connie walked in late on several occasions to be confronted by Dad sitting in his chair wearing the dreaded bathrobe.

Her philosophy about being late was simply "If I'm five minutes late, I'm late." So, she would walk into the house an hour late. Push!

There were several times when Connie was grounded. For the record, I was never grounded. In fact, I don't recall anyone else in the family being grounded, either. One time after yet another late arrival home, Mom and Dad gave her a small, yellow alarm clock to wear around her neck. The alarm clock was actually rather cute; not too big, but it made the point. In addition to wearing the clock, she was not allowed to leave the property. What did Connie do? She stood on the property line with one foot in front of the other. Push!

One time, Dad said, "A student can't get all As and get a C in conduct." Apparently, Connie took that as a personal challenge and did exactly that, all As and a C in conduct. Push!

Connie was also a very talented swimmer and fierce competitor. I loved being on a relay team with Connie, especially if we were behind and she was the anchor. I knew we couldn't lose, and we rarely did. She is tough – the 'won't back down' kind of tough. I have to admit there have been times during my life that I have admired Connie's type of toughness. No one pushes Connie around.

Moments that mattered with Connie taught me the following:

- There will always be members of the organization who are different and who don't want to conform. These individuals add great value to the organization. They do push back, they question what you are doing, and as a leader, they make you think. They don't always jump when asked.

BIRDIE

Birdie is #8 and the youngest girl. I am Birdie's older sister, enough older that I was the one she looked up to. I know there are times when I wasn't the best older sister. I'm sure I thought she was a pest, which is actually the role of a younger sister. I'm truly not sure I paid enough attention to Birdie growing up. In fact, I dated a boy who had a sister the same age as Birdie. I know I was kinder and paid more attention to her than to Birdie, and for that I am sorry. However, as we have grown older, our relationship has changed, and I have come to count on Birdie countless times in my adult life.

When my husband (Joe, more about him later) and I got married in 1982, there were not many dual military married couples. In fact, we only knew of one other. So, when our son Jay was born, we didn't know of any dual military couple with children, and one of the biggest challenges for us was childcare. In fact, I would often say that childcare was one of my biggest headaches and biggest heartaches. Thankfully, on more than one occasion, Birdie helped out in a big way with Jay.

The first time we called upon Birdie for help was when Jay was about nine months old. Joe had completed his master's degree at Georgia Tech and was heading to West Point, and I was in my summer quarter of graduate school at the University of Georgia. Birdie, a schoolteacher, came to Athens and spent six weeks of her summer vacation with me, helping with Jay. Those six weeks were wonderful and enabled me to get 'dug-in' in graduate school and set the conditions for my success. I didn't have to get Jay up early for daycare, and he was able to sleep in each day. He was with an aunt who took care of him and truly loved him. What was especially nice was that Birdie made dinner each day. I would walk into the apartment at the end of my day, and dinner would be ready.

It was wonderful, and it wasn't the last time that we called on Aunt Birdie to assist with Jay. Joe and I were selected to attend the Army's Command and General Staff College at Fort Leavenworth, Kansas. We arrived shortly after Jay turned four. There were a few women officers in the course who were dual-military, but I was the only one with a child. Initially, the course of instruction was going well, and then in early November we started tactics. Tactics is the way forces are deployed and utilized on the battlefield when engaging the enemy. I'm sure my Army buddies who read this will find this amusing, but tactics kicked my butt! I had never served in a unit where this was discussed and/or practiced.

Each day, Joe and I would take Jay to daycare on the way to Fort Leavenworth and spend the day in class. At the end of the day, we would pick Jay up and head home. Playtime, dinner, bath, brush, pray, and tuck Jay into bed. Then I would begin my studies, which was taking me into the wee hours of the morning. This had gone on for a few weeks, and I knew something had to give. On a Friday evening Joe and I had a talk and decided we would call Birdie to see if she could help out. We called her, and she was on a plane the next day, arriving to take Jay back to Olean. Birdie was still a schoolteacher there, and she arranged for a friend to watch Jay during the day while she cared for him in the evening.

Tactics didn't get easier. In fact, it got much harder, but I did have peace of mind knowing that Jay was loved and well cared for.

Moments that mattered with Birdie taught me the following:

- Sometimes in our lives we are reluctant to ask for help, yet there are people around us who are willing to give of their time and their talent. If you are busy, overwhelmed, and need help, ask. You may be surprised at the answer.

FAMILY TRADITIONS

Traditions are important. They keep us grounded in the world and in our lives. For our family, they bound us together in powerful ways. The first place I learned about the power of traditions was, of course, at home.

Mom always made holidays and birthdays very special, especially Christmas. My memories of Christmas are so numerous that they all come flooding into my head. I have always claimed that I remember a lot from my childhood, although I have been accused on occasion of making stories up. I would like to believe, though, that I have a better memory, especially since it appears that our parents intentionally worked to create lasting memories.

In our home the Christmas season would begin on Thanksgiving Day. Here are some of those memories and traditions. Watching the Macy's Parade on TV - Drawing names on Thanksgiving night – After Thanksgiving dinner going uptown to see the Christmas lights on

North Union Street - Looking for the perfect Christmas tree - Finding the perfect Christmas tree - The ubiquitous elves - Santa stamps in the bathroom - Yelling "Tell Santa I'll be good!" - Frosting and decorating Christmas cookies - Eating Christmas cookies – Matching Christmas aprons that Lala made for the girls - Singing Christmas carols - Buying the annual Firestone Christmas album - Hanging silver icicles on the tree, there were never enough - Opening one gift on Christmas Eve - new PJs - Hanging stockings - Dad reading *Twas the Night Before Christmas* - Trying to get Timer to wake up Christmas morning - Lining up to go downstairs youngest to oldest – Dad ringing the bell and saying, "I think he's been here." - Dad getting a potato in his stocking, every year and asking mom, "Do you think this is for me?"

And there were more! That special family gift, the tandem bike - Watching all of the Christmas specials - Red cherry Jell-O - Hawaiian Punch with 7-Up - The elf showing up at the bathroom window two years in a row! - Midnight Mass at the St. Bonaventure Chapel - The special blessing from the priest after Mass - Not being able to fall asleep Christmas Eve.

Here is one very, very special Christmas memory from my childhood. We were still living at 133 North Barry Street. It was the typical Christmas morning with lots and lots of excitement because Santa had definitely been there, but our presents were never wrapped. Mom said that there were too many, and it was too much wrapping for Santa and his elves. Instead, our gifts were in piles with some special gifts scattered around.

We would look for something that we had asked for and then would say to Mom, "Do you think this is for me?"

Mom would reply, "Is that something you asked for?"

If the answer was "Yes," then the pile of gifts was yours.

I never recall being disappointed on Christmas morning. I always enjoyed watching my brothers and sisters who would get so excited. The scream, "This is exactly what I wanted!" or a soft spoken, "Thank you Santa!" were comments heard often during the excitement of discovering wonderful and unexpected gifts.

One Christmas morning, Dad said, "Mo, will you go into the kitchen and get me a glass of water?" The kitchen door, the swinging type, was closed. I pushed it open and it swung shut behind me. As I walked into the kitchen there it was, a brand new, blue girl's bike with training wheels. Now, as much as I wanted that bike to be mine, I wasn't sure if it was, since I had not asked for a bike. But it might be, after all it was a girl's bike. But with five other girls in the house, it might be for Dee Dee, Connie or Birdie; Kathy and Judie no longer needed training wheels.

I sat on the bike, and as my luck would have it, it was a perfect fit! I sat there and thought, *I'm only going to sit on this bike for a minute.*

I was sure it was for one of my younger sisters, and at any time Mom or Dad would walk in and say, "Did you ask for that bike?"

I knew I hadn't, so I was going to sit and enjoy this brand new, blue, girl's bike with training wheels for a few more seconds. As I sat there imagining myself riding this bike on a warm spring day, I heard my dad.

"Mo, where is my water?" and the kitchen door swung open.

Time to get off the bike, I thought. Dad stood with a look of total surprise on his face.

"Where did this come from?" he asked with an excitement in his voice that was contagious.

"I don't know it was just in here." I asked my Dad who he thought the bike was for.

He responded with the anticipated question, "Did you ask for a bike?"

Oh, how I wanted to say yes, but I responded with an almost inaudible, "No."

Dad asked, "Do you need a bike?" to which I responded, "Yes!"

I had not thought about the fact that I didn't have a bike. Yes, I did indeed need a bike.

Dad said, "I think Santa left that bike for you!"

I was shocked and surprised! The bike was for ME!!! I didn't ask for a bike, but Santa knew that I needed one.

Later that day we went over to the indoor parking garage where I had the chance to ride my bike for the first time. During the next couple of years, I rode that bike everywhere, up and down Barry Street and then over on Clinton Street. Of course, I always got off and walked across the street; that was a rule. There is something unique and extraordinary about a first bike. It represented a sort of freedom, a moving into another stage of my life, training wheels and all.

Eventually the training wheels were going to come off. I practiced riding my bike a lot, and I wanted to ride a two-wheeler like the big kids, not a bike with training wheels. One summer day, I was around the block on Clinton Street riding bikes with friends. At one point, I got on my friend's bike, a two-wheeler, and started to pedal. I was a bit wobbly at first, but then as I began pedaling a bit faster, the wobbling stopped. I did it! I was riding without training wheels. I was so excited to get the training wheels off that I jumped on my bike and rode home. Breathlessly, I ran into the house and told my mom, "I can ride a two-wheeler!"

"Can you take the training wheels off my bike?" I asked.

My mother said, "I don't know how to do that. You will have to wait for your father to get home."

What? My mom who had a master's degree in chemistry didn't know how to use a wrench? I went into the garage and got a wrench. However, I didn't know how to use it either. I tried over and over again trying to figure out how to get those nuts loosened so I could release the training wheels.

This was probably the longest afternoon of my young life. I sat in the driveway continuing to try to figure out how to work that wrench. Finally, dad arrived home. I rushed up to him and told him my wonderful news. He walked out to the driveway with me, picked up the wrench, and began to go about the job of removing the nuts, bolts and washers. I watched my dad very closely, learning how to use the wrench.

Besides learning how to use a wrench, I realized much later in life that there was something else I learned that day. I learned that people, no matter who, can surprise us by what they can and cannot do.

It's a lesson that, to this day, still matters very much to me. Over the years I've learned not only how important it is to recognize and capitalize on the various strengths of my team members, but also to identify gaps or weaknesses and provide them with opportunities to improve.

Going back to the removal of the training wheels, I must say that, at the time, learning that my mom couldn't use a wrench was a shock; so much so that I decided right there and then that not only would I learn to use a wrench, but also that if I ever had a little girl, she would know how to use a wrench as well.

In fact, I did have that little girl, and one day when my daughter, Jackie, was ready to have her training wheels come off her bike, I went to my toolbox and pulled out a wrench. I told Jackie what I was going to do, and then I showed her. I took the wrench and placed it around the nut and then tightened it snugly, then rotated the nut left a few times, and it was released. One training wheel was removed from her bike. I then gave Jackie the wrench and had her (with a bit of help from me) loosen the nut, remove the washer and bolt, and release the other training wheel.

Since that day, Jackie and I have assembled and built countless items, and working on projects together has become somewhat of another of our family traditions. It's always fun when an item arrives and the words 'Assembly Required' are printed on the box. Jackie and I will look at each other, smile, pull out the red, metal toolbox, and get to work.

Years later, when Jackie was sharing an apartment with her cousin, Katie, she walked in as Katie and her mom, Dee Dee, were putting a dresser together. Jackie said, "I think you are putting that together wrong." She was right and helped her aunt and cousin take it apart and put the dresser together properly. That's my girl! She knows how to use a wrench!

One of the most powerful family traditions has been passed along by my mother. Mom wrote a letter each week, which we called 'the family letters.' Each week those who didn't live in the local area would call home to check in with Mom and Dad. Mom would then write a letter addressed to 'My Dearest Darlings.' The letter was a recap of each of our calls as well as information about those who lived locally. It kept us up to date on the rest of the family. Before mailing the letters, Mom would often pen an individual note around the margins. I have kept several years of family letters. They serve as a sort of family history. As you'll read further on in this book, you'll see how impactful letter writing can be from both a leadership and a personal standpoint. Sending a personal letter or hand-written note, among other things, is very important and shows you care.

Sometimes the strongest of traditions begin unexpectedly. My mother was born to my grandmother, Anna Finlay, on September 14, 1926 at St. Francis Hospital in Olean. She and my mother were released from the hospital on September 24th, ten days later. My grandmother had received several flower arrangements from friends and family over that time, and, believing that there were truly too many to take home, she had some delivered to the Sisters of Mercy convent, also located in Olean.

A few days later, she received a thank you note in the mail from one of the nuns. The flowers were a welcome surprise, and even more so because they arrived on the Feast of Our Lady of Mercy, which was an important day for the sisters. From that day on, my grandmother had flowers delivered to the convent each year on September 24th. When my grandmother passed away, my mother continued the tradition, until with the decrease in vocations to the Sisters of Mercy, the convent in Olean was closed. When the convent was closed, my mother instead had the flowers delivered each year to the Mercy Center in Buffalo.

My mother passed away in 2006, and I have carried on the tradition for our family. Each year when I send the flowers, I sign the card: 'From the children of Ann F. Keenan.' This tradition has endured for over 80 years.

My maternal grandmother, Anna, passed away six months before my mother and father married. I never knew her. However, I do know that she was a woman of incredible faith. While I never had the opportunity to meet Anna or call her Grandma, I feel a connection to her as I continue to carry on this tradition that she began. My daughter, Jackie, knows that at some point she will continue this tradition of sending flowers to the Sisters of Mercy on their feast day as well.

Traditions are important and can be powerful in helping families and organizations stay connected over the years and for generations. Families add new members through various ways. Organizations are constantly bringing on new hires. When a tradition is experienced for the first time, it is important that the reason behind the tradition be shared. This sharing or storytelling provides a sense of history and understanding. A new member can feel a sense of belonging and acceptance when traditions are both shared and understood.

CHAPTER TWO

DISCOVERING MORE MOMENTS THAT MATTERED

There are moments in our lives that can be significant and stick with us for a lifetime, like my wrench experience. Lessons such as these can fundamentally change the way we see ourselves and significantly influence how we choose to live our lives. Sometimes we recognize them at the time, and at other times, they result from our reflection on a certain event. I have some moments that I will share with you that were truly significant in my life and definitely made a difference.

FIRST GRADE – AN INTRODUCTION TO LEADERSHIP

When I was in first grade at St. Mary's School, if you lived close enough to school, you could walk home for lunch. As I was getting ready to head home one day for lunch, my teacher stopped me.

"Maureen, when you are home at lunch could you please ask your mother if you could stay after school? I would like you to represent our class at a meeting." On that day, Dad was also home for lunch. As I was eating my peanut butter and jelly sandwich, I remembered to ask Mom if I could stay after school.

My dad stopped eating, looked at me and said, "Mo Mo, a leadership position."

Two things stood out for me. First I had Dad's attention, which did not happen that often for me. And second, he said my name and the word leadership in the same sentence – that was a first for sure.

Later that day after school, I climbed the steps to one of the eighth-grade classrooms and took a seat at a desk that seemed enormous. I was representing my first-grade classmates. It was a moment that mattered. It was the first time I recall hearing the word 'leadership,' and in hindsight, I realize I was taking my first steps on a journey that would define my professional career – a journey of leading.

BECOMING A SWIMMER – THE RED RIBBON

One day when I was about six, Judie came home from a swim meet with a large, red ribbon. I remember standing around Dad's chair as he looked at it, turning it over in his hands. He then asked Judie to tell him how she had won her red ribbon. I stood there listening, fascinated not only that Judie won a ribbon, but also by Dad's response to her winning it. It was a red ribbon, a second-place finish, not first place, yet Dad made a big deal about Judie's performance. I could tell he was very proud of her.

As I stood there and watched the attention Judie was getting, I thought, *I can do that as well. I can swim.*

I also wondered how Dad would respond to a blue ribbon, a first place. The next day I got on my bike and rode to the Bartlett Country Club and joined the swim team.

This act, cued by the praise my sister received, began a swimming career that lasted through college, and had a significant impact on my life and my development as a leader. I was a fairly good swimmer and so there were numerous blue ribbons over the years. However, when I look back over those years of swimming, I realize it wasn't about the ribbons. As a swimmer, I learned so much: how to be a teammate, how to follow, how to work hard, how to lead, how to lose with dignity, and how to win with humility.

These were very important life-lessons, all sparked from a moment that mattered – Judie's winning of her red ribbon.

FOURTH GRADE – THE GOOD AND THE NOT SO GOOD

The order of nuns at St. Mary's were the (Sisters of) Mercy nuns. The head of the order in the region was referred to as Mother Superior. When I was in fourth grade, Mother Superior was scheduled to make a visit to our school. During the day, she was to visit each classroom. In preparation for her visit, we were told to stand and greet her upon her arrival and departure to our classroom. As I recall, she was not very tall and seemed quite old to me at the time, although I'm sure she was probably in her 40s!

Mother Superior had finished her visit and started to leave our classroom when she stopped, looked at us and said, "How many of you want to be President of the United States some day?"

Well, most of the boys raised their hands, and I did, too. I was the *only girl* who had raised her hand! My classmates sitting around me began giggling.

Mother Superior looked at me, pointed and said, "What is your name?"

I stood up and said, "Mother Superior, my name is Maureen Keenan."

She said to the rest of the class, "Don't laugh at Maureen. Some-day there will be a woman President."

I can't begin to explain how that moment felt. No doubt, I walked a little taller that day. Mother Superior validated me as someone who could be a leader. Of course, she was a leader in her order. It was a moment that I have thought of often over the years.

I had another fairly significant moment in fourth grade. It is a vivid memory; I even remember the date: December 6, 1963, the day before my birthday. It was the day I found myself in big trouble at school!

I was a well-behaved kid – I never caused any disciplinary concerns. I doubt there were too many discipline issues in Catholic grade schools back in the 1950s and 60s. In our family, if one of us had a discipline problem at school, he or she was going to have to explain it at home to Dad and probably receive an additional punishment. Double-jeopardy rules were not in place; Dad's rules took precedent. Additionally, if we were disciplined at school, the teacher in almost every case was supported by our parents.

In our fourth grade there were two classrooms, with approximately forty students in each room. Our desks were pushed together, two by two. My desk partner was not as obedient as I. He had done something and was told to stand in the doorway. The door was recessed, so as he stood there, the teacher couldn't see him, but I could.

He waved to me and I waved back in what I'm sure was merely a sign of solidarity. However, while the teacher couldn't see him, she saw me. In a flash she was standing in front of me, looking down. This particular teacher was a lay teacher, not a nun, but without hesitation she told me to go to the principal's office.

What!? I thought to myself. I was shocked at this request. I never, I mean never, was a troublemaker. Being sent to the principal's office was reserved for the most serious offenses. *Me! Mo Keenan! A kid who never was in trouble was being sent to the principal's office for waving!* I sat there actually stunned and speechless.

My teacher told me a second time to go to the principal's office, and I shook my head no. In hindsight, I should have gone to the principal's office. I probably would have been let off easy since I had never been in trouble. Maybe I could have helped the school secretary run off something on the mimeograph machine. As a result of my refusal to go to the principal's office, my teacher grabbed me and, yes, hit me a few times.

She then took me across the hall to the other fourth grade classroom. It wasn't bad enough that this happened in front of my class; now the other fourth graders saw me humiliated as well. When she opened the door, the face on the other fourth grade teacher was shock and surprise at seeing me. Did I mention that I never got in trouble? My teacher pushed me in front of a chalkboard and had me face the board. She departed the room.

The other teacher came over and said, "Maureen, what did you do?" I told her that I waved to someone.

She then said, "Well, we will have you stay with us for a while."

This incident happened close to the end of the school day. When the bell rang, I went back to my classroom and retrieved my books and coat. I had to tell someone what had happened, so I decided to tell my mom. I did ask, or maybe pleaded, for her not to tell Dad. She said she wouldn't tell him. That evening after dinner, Dad called me into the dining room.

He said, "I understand you had a problem at school today."

I wondered how he found out. Honestly, it never occurred to me that Mom told him. Anyway, I told him my side of the story.

He then said, "Maureen, obviously you did something that upset your teacher. Tomorrow, before school starts, I want you to go and apologize to her."

The next day, on my 10th birthday, I did as dad requested. Actually, it wasn't a request, it was a directive. Dad told me to apologize. I saw my teacher walk into school, waited a few minutes, gathered up my courage, went in and apologized. I don't recall how she responded.

Shortly after our first class started, she said she wanted everyone to turn in the Ten Commandments that they had to write one hundred times for homework the previous night. I panicked, not knowing what she was talking about. Eventually I realized that when she returned from taking me across the hall, the class was fooling around so they were punished with a writing assignment. December 6th turned out to be a bad day for everyone in our fourth grade.

This was a moment that mattered. Even though it wasn't a positive experience, I still learned quite a bit from this moment. I learned that sometimes people overreact to situations. I learned, too, that even those who don't ever get in trouble can, on occasion, have a no good, horrible, very bad day, and find themselves in trouble. Lastly, I learned that day that even when you don't think you are in the wrong, you still can apologize.

High School – Gaining Respect as a Leader

I was a cheerleader for three years in high school. I'm not sure why, but when I tell people, they seem to be amazed, shocked and surprised. However, when I was in high school, there were no athletics for girls outside of intramurals. Pre-title IX, there were no sports teams for the girls. Nevertheless, I loved sports. In our neighborhood during the summer, we played baseball and kickball. We played football in the fall and basketball in the winter months, and I suppose I was somewhat of a tomboy.

Admittedly so, I loved being a cheerleader as well! There, I said it. I loved the pom-poms, the cheers, and the uniforms. However, the uniforms we wore were very old. The junior varsity uniforms had been worn for well over a decade – probably longer. I had been the captain of the junior varsity cheerleaders and became captain of the varsity squad in my senior year.

While I was captain that senior year, I decided that we needed new uniforms. My plan: The varsity squad would get new uniforms and we would pass our uniforms to the junior varsity squad. I requested a meeting with the principal. To his credit, he met with me. I suppose that was because I was a good kid, never got in trouble again after fourth grade, and it probably didn't hurt that my mom taught at the same high school.

This was when I learned about the budget process in a school system. Who knew you actually had to plan for spending? During our meeting he opened up a rather thick document with a line for each item that was going to be purchased during the school year. We focused on the athletics department. I couldn't help but zero in on the line for the new wrestling mat, which was quite expensive. I knew the wrestling team already had a perfectly good wrestling mat because my boyfriend at the time was a wrestler. The principal explained to me that the items listed had already been ordered. However, new uniforms could be put in the budget for the next year. So, no new uniform for the squad my senior year. However, there would be new uniforms for the varsity cheerleaders the next year.

In that moment that mattered, actually it was more than a moment, I learned it is important for leaders to take the time to listen to and respect all members of an organization. The principal took the time to listen to me, a student. Additionally, I felt respected, especially when he actually showed me the budget. He didn't need to do that. I also learned that sometimes when you make something happen you may not benefit, but the organization will. This is called being a good steward. The cheerleaders were thrilled the next year when they got new uniforms. I was happy because I knew that I had helped make it happen.

One day the captain of the junior varsity cheerleaders asked if she could talk with me after practice. About fifteen minutes before practice ended, she walked in, sat down and watched. After practice ended, I walked over and asked what was on her mind.

She asked, "How do you do that?"

"How do I do what?" I replied.

She said, "Mo, they listen to you and there is no fighting."

In that moment, I realized that for some people, 'captain' is a title, and having a title does not mean all will listen. More importantly, not all will follow. Until that moment, it didn't occur to me that the girls on the squad wouldn't listen to me. I told her that she was the captain and she needed to take charge of her squad. I learned in that moment that mattered that, although some have leadership titles, they are not necessarily leaders.

ST. BONAVENTURE UNIVERSITY – RESPECT, DELEGATE, AND TRUST

Because my dad was a professor at St. Bonaventure University for fifty-two years, all nine of us had the opportunity to attend Bonas and are graduates. I knew in first grade that I was going to Bonas. In eighth grade as a cheerleader at St. Mary's, I decided that I would start growing my hair because all of the Bonas cheerleaders had long hair.

In the fall of my freshman year at St. Bonaventure, with my long hair in place, I tried out for cheerleading. I did, however, make a decision that if I didn't make the squad (which I knew wouldn't happen – *so confident with my long hair!*), I would join the women's swim team, which, as a result of Title IX, was established at St. Bonaventure my freshman year. The day of the cheerleading tryouts I was ready. I had practiced, I knew the cheers, my hair was long, and I wore the school colors, brown and white. I felt that I had a very good tryout. I was full of St. Bonaventure spirit!

Later that day the list with names of the St. Bonaventure cheerleading squad was posted. My name was not on the list. I didn't make the squad. Was I surprised that I didn't make the cheerleading squad? I was beyond surprised – I was devastated! Living home my freshman year, I reported to the family that I didn't make the cheerleading squad. Initially they thought I was kidding. In fact, one of my sisters actually drove to Bonas to look at the list. I'm not sure why I didn't make the squad, possibly because I lived at home and was unknown. Quite possibly because my dad was a professor at SBU, and people would say I only made the squad because my dad taught at SBU?

This was a moment that mattered. I had been planning to be a cheerleader at St. Bonaventure for four years. I had worked hard, and I was a very good cheerleader. I learned that even with planning and practice things don't always turn out the way we expect. Life is not always fair, and difficult things happen. It is good, however, to have a backup plan, and so I joined the swim team. We have all heard the saying, "When one door closes another door opens." I absolutely feel this was what happened with me when I joined the swim team because I thoroughly enjoyed being a member.

The first year the team was formed, most of the girls had never been competitive swimmers. Our coach asked for a show of hands of those who had previous competitive experience, and I was quite surprised that most had no experience. For many, the reason they were joining the team was to get into shape, although some of the girls with prior experience were quite good. Overall, we turned into a fairly competitive team. Not much was expected of us, and during the four years I was on the team, we experienced a fair amount, no, a large amount, of success. In the four seasons from 1972-76, we were 40-5-3.

On January 28, 1973 our team was invited to swim at Elmira College during the dedication of the Elmira College Athletic Education Center, a beautiful three-domed facility. We went into the locker room, changed, and then headed for the pool. It was time to warm up. I dove into the pool and the water was unbelievably cold – take your breath away cold! I recall that, after diving in the water and taking the first few strokes, I could barely breathe. I had been a competitive swimmer for years and could not recall ever swimming in such ice-cold water.

The NCAA actually has a rule that governs the temperature of the water for competitive swimming. It has to be at least seventy-seven degrees. The water temperature in the pool at Elmira was well below seventy-seven.

Coach gathered us around and said, "According to the rules, we don't have to swim today. The water is too cold. However, this is an important day for Elmira because they are dedicating their new athletic facility, and they have invited us to share in this event. The right thing for us to do today is swim."

On that day, I not only learned the water had to be a certain temperature for competitive swimming, but I also learned that it is important for leaders to talk to the folks they lead and help them understand the situation. Coach didn't have to sit us down and talk to us. He could have simply made the decision. Instead, he took a few minutes and explained what was going on, which made it easier for us to swim that day. It was still cold, but at the end of the day, I believe the Elmira team respected our team. We did the right thing!

In that moment that mattered, I recognized how important it is for a leader to talk to members of the organization and keep them informed. As a result of Coach talking with us, we didn't simply comply with coach's request. We were committed.

In my senior year at St. Bonaventure, I was elected team captain, and as you can imagine, I was pleased. Whenever I was on a team and eligible to be the captain, I wanted to be the captain. I recall one time when I was running for class office, I was unsure if it was right to vote for myself.

Dad said, "Do you think you are the best one for the job? If the answer is yes, vote for yourself."

I always voted for myself.

Being the team captain of the women's varsity swim team for me was a big deal. Shortly after I was selected as captain, the coach asked me to meet him in his office. He congratulated me and then handed me two checklists. One was all of the tasks that had to be accomplished before every home swim meet, and the other was for away meets. As I thumbed through the checklists, I asked him how I was to get all of this accomplished before each meet.

He said, "Maureen, this is when you learn to delegate and trust your teammates." I hadn't recalled ever having an issue with any of the girls on the team. We had no drama. In that moment that mattered, I knew that I would delegate tasks and could trust my teammates.

I experienced several other moments that mattered that year, and I learned that leadership was much more than delegating. We had our last home swim meet. It was my senior year, and the season was over. I was sitting in a chair poolside when one of the freshmen swimmers came out of the locker room and said, "Mo, thanks for being such a good team captain."

She went on to tell me that all her life she had been a very good swimmer and had always received a lot of attention from her coaches. When she arrived at St. Bonaventure, this was not the case. While she was an excellent swimmer, there were several other girls who were quite good as well. Additionally, our coach wasn't the type of person to give special attention to any one swimmer.

She continued, "You always came up to me before and after every race."

I'm not sure that this was anything that I ever consciously thought I needed to do because I was the captain; it was just something I did. However, for this young swimmer it was important. In that moment that mattered, I learned that even small gestures do make a big difference for members of the organization.

Two of my younger sisters, Dee Dee and Connie, were also on the women's swim team at St. Bonaventure when I was the captain.

A year after I graduated from college, my sister Dee Dee said, "I didn't know what a good team captain you were until you were gone."

This was high praise, especially when it was coming from a younger sister. In that moment that mattered, I learned that sometimes positive feedback comes from the most unexpected individual in the organization.

CHAPTER THREE

MY ARMY JOURNEY – PART 1

FINDING MY PATH

My journey into the United States Army began when I was an undergraduate student at St. Bonaventure University. During my sophomore year, the Reserve Officer Training Corps (ROTC) program began accepting women. I immediately joined the program. Timer was in the Army, and as I mentioned earlier, I held him in high regard and felt that joining the Army was something I would enjoy. And enjoy it I did! We fired weapons, rappelled, went on field training exercises, ate c-rations, and actually flew in a UH-1 (Huey) helicopter! It was a thoroughly interesting, and most times, thrilling, experience for me that year.

Unfortunately, there was a portion of my experience that wasn't so thrilling. Before I was to begin my junior year, I had to have a military medical physical examination to continue in ROTC. My physical examination was scheduled, but I didn't show up for it.

My dad was not only on the faculty at St. Bonaventure, he was also an officer in the United States Air Force Reserves. To say he was a big supporter of the ROTC program was putting it mildly. When I did not show for my physical, one of the ROTC instructors called

Dad, who tracked me down and was quite angry with me. Since he found out from someone else that I didn't show up for my physical, Dad was both embarrassed and irritated.

He said, "I have egg on my face."

I told Dad that I had decided I didn't want to continue in the ROTC program, which was not true, but at the time, I truly was not ready to go through with the physical examination.

Quite honestly, this is not a story that I have shared with many people. And to understand the real reason I did not show up for my military medical physical exam that year, we need to go back in time a bit.

When I was four months old, a blemish began to appear on my right index finger that proceeded to spread up my arm and stopped slightly short of my elbow. When this appeared on my arm, my parents took me to a dermatologist in Buffalo. My mother took me in to see the doctor alone as Dad had the four older kids in the car.

Years later, when Mom shared the story of that doctor visit, she said that when the doctor saw my arm, he invited several other doctors into the room to look at my arm. Apparently, I had a condition that most of those doctors had not previously seen. My mother was standing outside of the circle of doctors as they examined my arm, and listening in on the doctors' conversations, she was convinced I had cancer and they were going to amputate my arm. When Dad picked us up, Mom was crying. I can't begin to imagine how stressful that visit was for her.

Fortunately, it was not cancer. The medical term for what I have is epidermal nevus. Basically, it is abnormal, noncancerous skin caused by an overgrowth of cells. The best way to describe my epidermal nevus is that it was a raised, red rash. In the winter my arm would get extremely dry, itch, crack and bleed. Each night as I would get ready for bed, I would slather Vaseline™ all over my arm and then cover it with a sock.

At some point my parents decided that I should have plastic surgery on my arm to remove the epidermal nevus. They actually took me to a photographer and had pictures taken of my arm so that when I was older, they could explain the reason for the surgeries and, more importantly, show me what my arm looked like before the surgeries. I probably had five or six operations on my arm.

As a result of my surgeries I was afraid, no, *terrified*, of doctors. The doctor who performed my surgeries was our family doctor, a general practitioner. He was the same doctor who was there for all nine births, set our bones, sutured our wounds, and performed various surgeries, including my plastic surgery. He was also my godfather. He was a bit gruff, to say the least. One day my younger brother, Kevin, saw him walking down the street and gave him a ride. Upon reaching his destination he thanked Kevin and got out of the car.

Kevin said, "Have a nice day!"

Our family doctor leaned in the car and replied, "I hate that expression." So yes, he was a bit gruff.

One of my surgeries is still quite memorable. It was January 20, 1961, the day President Kennedy was inaugurated, and I was in first grade at the time. I have a vivid memory of shopping with my mom before my surgery. Together we purchased new pajamas, fuzzy slippers and a light blue bathrobe. Shopping alone like this with Mom was very unusual and, yes, very special. My surgery was scheduled early in the morning, but since I was so afraid of the doctor and the hospital, Mom brought me to the hospital as late as she could the night before. We arrived at St. Francis Hospital sometime after dinner. Mom got me into my hospital gown and settled me into the bed.

A young nurse came in who said she needed to shave my leg. I told her they were operating on my arm, and she responded by telling me they were taking skin off my leg. She began shaving my upper thigh. My mom didn't say anything, and I simply assumed this nurse had the incorrect room. I was wrong. Skin was to be taken off my right thigh and put on the knuckle on my right index finger and wrist. Apparently, as a little girl I was a worrier, so Mom and Dad had decided not to tell me about the skin graft.

I woke up early the morning of my surgery, and I was homesick. It was quiet in the hospital, and in January in Olean, you can count on it to be dark outside at that hour. I thought about the activity that was going on at home as my brothers and sisters prepared for school. The morning ritual was pleasantly consistent and grounding: various brands of cereal being poured into bowls, slices of bread being toasted and buttered, and lunches being made and put into brown paper bags labeled with names. A call would be made upstairs to make sure everyone, especially Connie, was up and moving. Of course, the local radio station, WHDL, would be playing in the background. Soon however, Dad walked into my room, and then shortly thereafter, I was moved from my bed onto the gurney and wheeled into the operating room.

Olean is a small town. The anesthesiologist lived around the block from our house. He was a kind man. As he prepared me for anesthesia, he told me to look at the machine that he used to control the levels of ether. There were two glass tubes. They had markings, and inside each tube was something that looked like a small gold bullet. He told me the Lone Ranger had given those bullets to him. I laughed, he gently placed the ether mask over my face, and I was out.

I woke in the recovery room. There were other patients in the recovery room as well, along with several nurses. Many of the nurses at St. Francis were nuns who wore all-white habits. I looked to my right and noticed a woman patient, who at that very moment rolled over, exposing her bare bottom. I was six, so this was funny, and I laughed. One of the nuns walked over, covered the woman's bottom, clicked her tongue and gave me a look. I then began to gag. A typical response after ether is throwing up. The nun told me she could give me a shot. I told her I didn't need a shot.

After a short time, I asked the nun if I could walk back to my room. She told me I couldn't walk because I had my leg operated on. *What?* Evidently, that young nurse did know what she was doing. When I was finally wheeled back to my room, we went past a waiting room where there was a television. Mom and Dad were sitting in the room watching young President Kennedy's inauguration address. This was the last surgery I had on my right arm.

Since then, doctors, nurses, hospitals, and shots all continued to terrify me. A nurse once told me how brave I was because I wasn't crying. I wasn't brave, I was terrified! I was beyond scared and couldn't even cry. One time we were at the Cattaraugus County Fair and there was a nurse at a display. I ran away because I thought she was going to give me a shot. If someone had on white shoes, I was convinced that he or she was a doctor or nurse. If we were going for a ride and I thought we might drive past St. Francis Hospital, I would quickly look in the car to see if my little suitcase was there. I worried that we would pull in and I would have to have an operation, even though Mom and Dad always told me when I was having surgery.

Growing up, I honestly didn't experience too many comments about my arm, but there were a few. One day as I played with a friend she said, "Is that catchy?"

I didn't know what she meant so I asked, "What do you mean by catchy?"

"Can I get it if I touch it?" she asked.

In that moment I realized that she didn't like how my arm looked and certainly didn't want it on her. Almost without hesitation I said, "Yes!" While at the same time I rubbed my arm across her face. She ran off crying.

One summer when I was about ten years old, I was getting ready for swim team practice. Coach looked at my arm and said, "Mo, what happened to your arm over the winter?"

At first, I didn't know what he was talking about, so I looked at my arms. Then I realized that, while I had been a swimmer for him for several years, he had never noticed my scar. I said, "Oh, that's not new, I have had it all my life."

Swimmers tend to become lifeguards, and I was no exception. During my college years I spent a couple of summers as a head lifeguard and assistant manager at our local public swimming pool. I was on deck talking to a guy who was a couple of years younger, and he said, "Your arm looks like a piece of shit!"

My response? None! I was speechless.

What is interesting is that when you have a scar like mine, it becomes part of who you are. I have always had this scar on my right arm from the tip of my index finger to my elbow. I don't think it's ugly, I've never covered it up, never deliberately worn long sleeves. I kind of like my scar, it is a part of me. It is part of my story.

Back to the reason for my failure to show up for my Army physical – I was still so terrified! This was to be a full medical physical, and there were some aspects of the examination that were going to be done to me that I had never experienced. I knew shots might possibly be involved and there would be gynecological and rectal exams. I know! I know! I was in college, I should have been more mature, brave too, but it was overwhelming. I absolutely was not ready.

The following year, as I walked through the Reilly Center (the student union), I saw a woman Army officer at a desk. I was on my way to swim practice and did not have time to stop. After practice as I passed the desk, the officer was gone. However, she left some brochures behind. I took one of each, went back to my dorm room and read the information. The brochures contained details about applying for the Women's Army Corps Student Officer Program. Before ROTC and the United States Military Academy were open to women, this program was a way for women to become Army officers. The next day I gave her a call.

I know what you are thinking – she has to have a military physical exam – but I wanted to go into the Army. The physical was scheduled in Buffalo at the military processing center. Yes, I was nervous, so Mom went with me, and we spent the night in a hotel. I managed to get through the physical.

I attended the four-week training program at Fort McClellan in Alabama during the summer between my junior and senior years in college. There were about 125 women from all over the country; eighty-five would be selected to go on active duty after we graduated from college. We were evaluated in physical training, obstacle courses, marksmanship and several other subjects that focused on the Army. As part of the selection process, a panel of women officers interviewed us. Shortly after returning home, I received a letter that I had been selected to go on active duty upon graduation.

This was a moment that mattered. I picked up those brochures, and that simple action changed the course of my life.

My First Assignment and Meeting Captain Right

On May 23, 1976 I raised my right hand and took the oath that every commissioned officer in the United States Army takes.

"I do solemnly swear that I will support and defend the Constitution of the United States against all enemies, foreign and domestic; that I will bear true faith and allegiance to the same; that I take this obligation freely, without any mental reservation

or purpose of evasion; and that I will well and faithfully discharge the duties of the office on which I am about to enter. So help me God."

With that, I was a second lieutenant in the United States Army.

Upon completing my initial officer training, I was assigned to Fort Eustis in Virginia, the home of the Army's Transportation Corps. I recall vividly the day I drove onto Fort Eustis in my white MGB, and I wondered to myself, *What will this assignment be like,* and, *Will I make new friends?*

My first job was as a logistics staff officer with the 7th Transportation Group. I worked with two seasoned sergeants first class. They had never worked with a woman soldier, they didn't care, and they were great. One day they walked in my office and gave me a set of olive drab Army issue coveralls and said, "Lieutenant, tomorrow we go to the motor pool."

Of course, I took those coveralls home, washed and, yes, pressed them. I wanted to look sharp. The next day we drove in a jeep and entered the motor pool. I often wondered what we looked like as we hopped out of the jeep. Two crusty (I use that term affectionately) non-commissioned officers (NCOs) in their wrinkled, grease-smeared coveralls and me, the second lieutenant, looking like it was her first time in an Army motor pool, which of course it was. On that day they taught me how to conduct a technical inspection (TI) on a two-and-a-half-ton truck, which was referred to as a deuce-and-a-half.

At one point during the TI, I was under the vehicle on a dolly, and I heard one of the sergeants say, "Hello, Sir!"

When one is a second lieutenant, all other officers outrank you. I quickly rolled myself out from under the vehicle, jumped up, and saluted. It was Colonel Piner, the commander of the 7th Transportation Group. I introduced myself, and soon he moved on.

The military has a lot of traditions, and one of those is an event called the Hail and Farewell. At this function, new members of the organization are welcomed, and those departing are thanked for their contributions to the organization and given a gift.

The colonel I had previously met in the motor pool presided over the Hail and Farewell, and when it was my turn to be hailed, he said, "The first time I met LT Keenan, she was in the motor pool wearing coveralls and coming out from under a deuce-and-a-half. That is exactly what young lieutenants should be doing."

I realized in that moment that 'doing' was important in the Army. Of course, I was thankful to the two sergeants who taught me that valuable lesson.

One of the aspects I have always liked about serving in the Army was that I wasn't tied to a desk. There were always opportunities to get out of the office. Another lesson I learned was leadership sometimes could be acquired by walking around. The group commander was always out and about, checking on his organization.

After spending some time on the 7th Transportation Group staff, I had the opportunity to become a platoon leader, so in January 1978, I was transferred to the 558th Transportation Company. One of the other companies in that battalion was the 497th Engineer Company. Later that year, Captain Joseph LeBoeuf arrived to take command of the 497th. I knew that there was a new commander of the engineer unit; however, I had not yet seen him. At the Hail and Farewell, Captain LeBoeuf was introduced.

As the commander talked about him, I thought, *There's another loser engineer.*

When I was on the 7th Transportation Group staff, I had had a lot of interactions with Captain LeBoeuf's predecessor, who I thought was totally incompetent. So, yes, I admit that I judged him and put him in a category before I even met him or saw him work.

It turned out that Joe LeBoeuf, a West Point graduate, class of 1974, was absolutely the sharpest officer I had ever seen. His uniform was impeccable, boots highly shined, and when I saw him in meetings, he was always extremely well prepared. A fellow officer once described him by saying, "He looks like new money every day."

Professionally, I admired him. At this particular point in time, I was in a relationship with an Army officer who was in flight school at Fort Rucker in Alabama, so I was not looking at Captain LeBoeuf in a romantic or in any way other than a professional manner. Another thing I noticed about Captain LeBoeuf was that he always carried a nice pen, not the black military issue pen that most of us used. Instead, he carried a silver Cross® pen. My dad was a 'pen guy,' so I suppose that was why I noticed.

One day I attended a meeting on behalf of my company commander with our battalion commander, and he asked Captain LeBoeuf a question.

Captain LeBoeuf was holding his pen and said, "Sir, I don't believe your staff has properly briefed you."

Two observations here: first, I loved the way he held the pen and used it to make a point; and second, he was basically telling the battalion commander he was wrong. I had never seen this, so I was quite impressed.

One Sunday I was at mass and I noticed Captain LeBoeuf coming back from Communion.

Hmmmm, I thought, *Captain LeBoeuf is Catholic.*

The person I was dating was Southern Baptist. While I thought that I was going to marry him, the religious difference was a point of stress in our relationship. I am a practicing Catholic, and although he was Southern Baptist, he never went to church. On more than one occasion we talked about children and how they might be raised. He thought we could go to mass one week and the Baptist service the next. I believed that children should have a strong foundation in one faith and when they are older can make their own decision. Also, since he never went to church, I wasn't sure how the 'every other week plan' would work. I decided to talk to a priest.

As I walked into the building where the Catholic Chaplain had his office, the religion classes were being dismissed. In that moment I realized that so many of the wonderful memories I had from my childhood centered around the Catholic Church. Attending Catholic school at St. Mary's from kindergarten through 8th grade and then attending St. Bonaventure; not to mention, Baptisms, First Holy Communions, Confirmations, Christmas Eve Mass, Holy Week, and Easter Sunday made for so many pleasant memories. While the relationship did not end immediately, this was probably the moment when I realized that I would not marry him.

Another tradition in the Army is Officers' Call, which is a gathering of all of the officers of the unit at a specified location. The purpose of Officers' Call is to build unit cohesion, camaraderie and esprit-de-corps. Oh, and drinking is usually involved. We had mandatory Officers' Call at the Officers' Club (O Club) each Wednesday after work. There were strippers at the O Club, yes, strippers! It was an interesting time for women in the Army, and I'm sure for the women in other military services as well. It was mandatory we attend Officers' Call, no excuses; everyone showed up. I always attended and would sit at a table with my fellow platoon leaders with my back to the strippers.

Did I ever speak out against this? No! I was a young lieutenant, and I'm convinced that if I had spoken up, nothing would have happened other than my career ending sooner than I would have wanted. I have talked to other women officers who had similar experiences when they first came on active duty, and they didn't say anything either. Eventually the strippers were gone from the O Clubs.

One week at an Officers' Call, I was talking to one of my fellow platoon leaders, and we talked about everything, including relationships. He knew that the relationship I was in was probably not the best for me.

He said, "I think you should start dating other guys."

About thirty minutes later Captain Joe LeBoeuf asked me out, and I said, "Yes."

After our first date, I walked into my apartment, sat down and wrote a 'Dear John' letter. Following our three-and-a-half-year courtship, Joe and I were married in the chapel at St. Bonaventure University. The day I first drove on to Fort Eustis I wondered what new friends I would make. I never dreamed that I would meet my best friend, life partner and biggest cheerleader.

Flight School

When I was training at Fort McClellan as a young lieutenant, an officer arrived from Personnel Command to discuss the various branches and specialty schools available to us. Flying always fascinated me, and I thought it would be something I'd like to do.

Unfortunately, when asked about the prospects of any of us attending flight school, he answered, "None of you will ever attend flight school."

At the time, I'm sure this was the truth. The Army probably had enough pilots. A few years later, however, that truth changed.

One day while stationed at Fort Eustis, a fellow platoon leader mentioned that he was going to take the flight aptitude test.

I said, "I was told we would never go to flight school."

He responded, "Maureen, they can't stop you from applying."

Inspired, I went ahead and took all of the necessary tests, a flight aptitude exam and flight physical. I completed the necessary paperwork and submitted a packet to Personnel Command to be considered for flight school.

A few months later, my phone rang. It was my assignment officer at Personnel Command who asked if I could get to Fort Rucker to attend flight school in six weeks. He went on to say that an officer who was slated to attend was no longer able to go. I told him I was going to have to talk to my boss and would call him the next day. My boss said yes, and so the next day I called my assignment officer and told him I could go to flight school!

In July 1979, I reported to the Army's rotary wing flight school located at Fort Rucker, Alabama. I graduated flight school in April 1980 and was the sixty-eighth woman to become an Army aviator. I know my number because we were told.

Flight school was interesting. The first phase of flight school was in a TH-55 helicopter, three blades on the main rotor. It accommodated two, the instructor pilot (IP) and the student. In a helicopter, the command pilot sits in the right seat. During this initial phase, there were three students assigned to an instructor pilot. Both of the other two student pilots, or my 'stick buddies,' had flying experience. One, an Army officer, had his fixed wing private pilot's license. The other, a graduate of the United States Air Force Academy, had flying and glider experience. I had no flying experience at all, except for being a passenger in commercial aircrafts and the orientation ride we had in the Huey during ROTC at St. Bonaventure.

Our IP was a retired Army Warrant Officer with thousands of hours of flight time. He was a gruff individual who always chewed dip. He actually carried a spit cup in the lower leg pocket of his flight suit.

He had never taught a woman how to fly, and the first day we met he said, "Don't think I'm going to treat you differently because you are a girl."

I smiled.

The major accomplishment during the initial part of flight school is soloing the aircraft. As a part of our uniform in flight school, we wore baseball caps. Each flight class had its own unique color cap; ours was a light blue. After successfully soloing the TH- 55, we were authorized to have a set of wings sewn on our hats above our rank. The fact that someone had soloed was on display for all to see. My stick buddies had soloed. I asked them how they knew when they were going to solo. They told me the IP would swear. He had never used any foul language with me. However, one day we were flying, and he over rolled the throttle, and the tail rotor of the aircraft kicked a bit.

He said, "What the *(expletive deleted)* are you doing?"

I responded, "I didn't do anything. You did that." Then I thought, *I'm going to solo!*

He had me land the aircraft. He got out and said, "Take it around the pattern three times." I soloed!

As a part of the assessment of how the student pilots are performing, ten percent check rides were given. Flight examiners from the assessment branch of the flight school would fly with the student pilots to make sure they were progressing. It was also a way to evaluate the IPs. These check rides were referred to as ten percent rides because they evaluated ten percent of any given class. Of course, I was selected. My check pilot came strutting into the room. Oh yes, if there existed a stereotype for a pilot, he was it. Good looking (He knew it!) and cocky.

The check rides took several hours. It started at a table where a lot of questions were asked about the aircraft and flying in general. Next, we had to pre-flight the aircraft, and more questions were asked. It was summer, so the doors of the aircraft were off. We were flying along, and the aircraft was out of trim, essentially not as straight as it could have been. The check pilot said, "You are out of trim, but I don't care because I like the smell of your perfume."

The flight had gone well, we had finished the flight, and I was hovering to my parking place. I was literally a few feet away. There was a gust of wind and the check pilot grabbed the controls. I didn't lose control of the aircraft and was unsure why he took that action. Of course, I knew that because he touched the controls, I had busted my check ride and was given a pink slip. Essentially, it's like failing a big test.

My IP was quite bothered when I busted the check ride. No doubt he was concerned that he was treating me differently, and maybe I wasn't progressing as well as he thought. I was unaware of this at the time. My IP was absent the next time I flew, so I assigned to another IP. It was a normal flying session, not much different than what I was experiencing with my own IP.

We had landed the aircraft, and as I was hovering into position to takeoff, the IP said, "I want you to perform a max performance takeoff."[8] So, I did.

He said, "That was excellent!"

"Thanks! It's the first one I've ever done." I said.

---

[8] A max performance takeoff is performed in a space where obstacles might be in the way.

I could tell he was surprised. He asked how I knew how to do it, and I told him that I read about the procedure. At the end of that day I received great feedback from the substitute IP.

At the conclusion of each phase of flight school, you have to take and pass a check ride. My check pilot was a big man, very nice and, more importantly, respectful. When we had finished, we returned to the classroom to receive our feedback and find out if we had passed. After the check pilot finished talking with me and told me I had passed, he asked me a question.

"Were you the student who flew with so-and-so for the ten percent check ride?"

I said, "Yes."

He then went on to say, "So, Lieutenant, how did it feel to be screwed with your pants on?"

A little crude yes, but I realized that I shouldn't have failed that check ride, and others knew it as well.

Flight school was full of memorable moments – some good and some not so good. On one hand there was my IP who wanted to make sure he didn't treat me any differently, and then the check pilot who absolutely treated me differently because I was a girl.

Once we completed our initial entry phase of flight school, we changed airframes and flew the UH-1H. This is the helicopter you see in all the Vietnam films. I had an IP who was an Army captain and West Point graduate. He was never very friendly, and I was well aware that he didn't like me. One day we were flying and coming in for an approach. He told me to perform the simulated hydraulic power failure. If you have ever tried to steer a car with the hydraulics off, this was similar. It required some strength. I worked out every day in flight school, running and was pumping a lot of iron.

As he reached up and turned off the hydraulic circuit breaker, he said to me, "Don't think I'm going to help you because you are a girl."

"Sir, I didn't ask for your help," I countered, and then I proceeded to successfully land the aircraft.

FAILURE AND NOT QUITTING

I worked hard in flight school, but it was not easy for me. As mentioned earlier, I had never flown before, so it was all totally new. I was progressing and doing okay; not great, just okay. When we began the instrument phase however, I struggled from the start. It was difficult for me to visualize what I was doing while using only the instruments. Upon reflection, I probably needed to learn this through a different method.

I didn't let anyone know how much I was struggling, and then came my check ride. I busted my check ride and then had to spend time with another IP. I started to fall behind the rest of my class, and then I busted a second check ride. By this point I had a couple of options. One option was to join the class behind ours, another was to leave flight school. I decided I would leave. Yes, I decided to quit flight school.

I called home to tell my parents I was leaving flight school. I'm sure I cried when I told them I didn't want to do it anymore. I had already started the process of visiting all of the offices to get my paperwork signed so that I could leave. One evening my phone rang, and it was my brother, Bob.

He never called, and not beating around the bush, he said, "Keenans don't quit!"

It was precisely the kick in the butt I needed. I decided to stay and finish what I had started. I was put into another class—I was now in the green hat class. The members of the class were nice enough, but

I had not been with them from the start, so I never totally integrated with them. Interestingly, the class I had been with quit socializing with me. We had been together for months, worked out together almost daily, went to dinner together and partied together. They moved on without me. It was as if something was wrong with me and they didn't want to get too close. While I was with the green hat class, there were some interesting moments, and one is quite memorable.

Streaking

Back in the spring of 1974, streaking had become a craze on college campuses around the country, including at St. Bonaventure. There would be reports of sightings, such as, "a streaker ran into the campus post office," or "a streaker ran through Hickey Dining Hall." The streaker sightings were reported on the SBU radio station.

One day the DJs said that there was going to be a mass streaking on campus that night. I didn't live on campus, but I was on campus that night. Cheering students lined up, and all of a sudden what seemed like hundreds of masked and unmasked students came running out of one of the dorms naked.

My dad, being well known in the local community, was often approached by people who would ask, "What is going on at St. Bonaventure?"

Dad's response was, "They are engaging in college pranks, not hurting anyone. They are not burning buildings." (In 1970, two barns on campus *were* burned to the ground. Those who burned the barns were never identified.)

When the students streaked, Dad believed these events were simply college kids engaging in college pranks; harmless in comparison with what went on in 1970. I never recall any comments or actions by the administration, and after a few weeks the streaking fad ended. It would become one of the topics of conversation each time we gather for class reunions – a memory shared.

While the streaking fad was occurring at St. Bonaventure and at colleges around the country, it was being talked about at West Point as well. In fact, the cadet DJs on the USMA radio station, WKDT, reported one evening that there was going to be a streaker at West Point. The rumor going around was that a cadet was going to streak in the school's Central Area, which is the area surrounded on all sides by the cadet barracks.

At West Point, the Corps of Cadets (the student body) is made up of approximately 4,400 cadets. There are four regiments, and each regiment has eight lettered companies, A to H. Each company is comprised of cadets from each of the four classes. During his time as a student there, my husband, Joe, was assigned to A-1. Each of the companies had a motto. A-1's motto was 'Be Straight or Be Gone.' This implied that one must be totally squared away, very sharp. Joe fit that image, always looking good in his uniform. He set a high standard for himself.

Cadets are college-age students, and while this may come as a surprise to some, cadets don't always do the right thing; they get into trouble. When they get in trouble, demerits are assigned. Once a certain number of demerits is reached, a cadet has to walk them off. These cadets form up, are inspected by the Officer in Charge, and walk for a prescribed number of hours around the perimeter of the Central Area on Fridays and Saturdays. Some cadets are members of the Century Club, meaning they have walked over one hundred hours. Joe earned only a few demerits while at West Point, and he never walked the area.

As a firstie[9], Joe was selected to be the First Regimental Commander. Those selected are sharp cadets who are doing well in the academic, military and physical programs. It was a big deal to be selected.

---

[9] A firstie is a senior at West Point.

63

The Commandant of Cadets (similar to the Dean of Students) had the senior cadet leadership report to his office. They were the First Captain, the cadet who is in charge of the entire Corps of Cadets, and the four Regimental Commanders. The Commandant told them they were to stand watch and catch the streaker.

After the meeting, Joe told the First Captain, "Jack, this is bullshit!"

However, being good cadets, they did as they were asked.

Joe and another firstie were standing, looking out a window. The cadets were hanging out of their windows cheering, waiting for the streaker. Joe and the other cadet looked at each other and smiled, no words were exchanged. They went to their rooms, got their Converse sneakers and skullcaps, and met back in the basement. Another cadet saw them and immediately knew what was going to happen, and joined in.

They stripped down, laced up their sneakers, put on the skullcaps and ran into the Central Area. To the cheering and clapping of hundreds or probably thousands of cadets with arms raised, they ran around for a few minutes and then disappeared back into the barracks where they quickly dressed, no one the wiser, or so they thought.

The Commandant was furious. He wanted to know the names of the cadets and wanted them punished. Apparently, the cadets knew the identity of the streakers; however, it was not verified. The Commandant wanted the names. He called in the First Captain, and he wanted the streakers expelled from the Military Academy.

The First Captain, Jack Pattison, a Vietnam vet and the oldest member of the Corps of Cadets, was well respected by the Commandant and asked the Commandant if he could handle the situation. Reluctantly, the Commandant agreed. Jack walked into Joe's room; he didn't directly ask Joe if he was one of the streakers.

Joe said, "So what's the punishment?"

Jack said, "You are on room confinement for 30 days."

Shortly after the streaking incident, Joe received an anonymous letter from a fellow cadet. The cadet wrote that he was glad to see a cadet leader at West Point take such a risk and do something so out-side of what was expected within the strict, rigid environment where they were all required to act a certain way. Certainly there were other cadets who must have felt the same way.

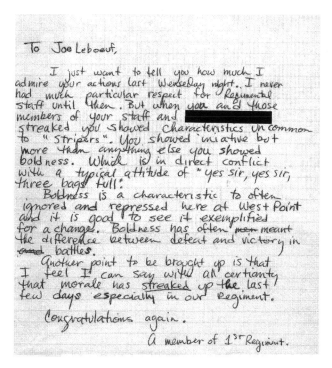

To Joe Leboeuf,

I just want to tell you how much I admire your actions last Wednesday night. I never had much particular respect for Regimental staff until then. But when you and those members of your staff and ▮▮▮▮▮▮ streaked you showed characteristics uncommon to "Stripers". You showed initiative but more than anything else you showed boldness. Which is in direct conflict with a typical attitude of "yes sir, yes sir, three bags full".
   Boldness is a characteristic to often ignored and repressed here at West Point and it is good to see it exemplified for a change. Boldness has often meant the difference between defeat and victory in battles.
   Another point to be brought up is that I feel I can say with all certianty that morale has streaked up the last few days especially in our Regiment.

Congratulations again.

                    A member of 1st Regiment.

One evening at flight school while I was in the green hat class, I was on the bus headed to the flight line for a night flight. I was sitting next to a classmate whom I didn't know very well. He introduced himself, and we struck up a conversation.

At one point he asked, "Are you dating anyone?"

I said, "Yes."

He then asked, "Is he an Army officer?"

"Yes." I replied.

"Where did he go to school?" He asked.

"He's a West Point graduate."

He went on with questions, "What's his name?"

I said, "Joe LeBoeuf."

He responded with great excitement in his voice, "I know Joe, we streaked together at West Point!"

My response, "Really?!"

The next day I called Joe. I said, "Joe, one of my classmates is a West Point grad and he said he knows you."

Joe said, "Really, what's his name?"

I replied with the name of his fellow streaker.

There was silence at the other end of the phone.

I honestly could not imagine Joe LeBoeuf streaking. It isn't outside the box for him – it's way outside the box.

Now, I'm not suggesting that we take off our clothes and streak; however, leaders do need to be a bit outrageous at times. Sometimes it's okay to keep people wondering. I believe that being a bit outrageous at times might allow those you lead to be more creative and innovative.

I did continue with the green hat class and graduated from flight school; I earned my wings, and I'm glad I didn't quit. I have had a lot of difficult experiences in my life, and for me, flight school was very difficult. It was one of those life experiences that I have looked back on from time to time and have thought, *I did that; I can do this.* After all, Keenans don't quit!

GERMANY

My first assignment as a pilot was in Nellingen, Germany. I was the second woman officer assigned to an aviation maintenance battalion. The first woman had arrived a few weeks prior. I didn't know her, but I knew of her. We were in flight school at the same time. She was the first African-American woman to graduate from flight school, and when she graduated, there was an article about her in the Fort Rucker post paper that focused on the historic nature of the first African-American woman to graduate from flight school. Additionally, her IPs all commented on her great skills as a pilot.

When you arrive at a new military organization, there is a tremendous amount of in-processing to be done. However, when you are a pilot, you also have to get checked out in your aircraft. Basically, you have to go on check rides with the pilots who are trained flight examiners. The other woman officer began her flying and busted her check ride. Each time she went out, she was failed. I wasn't sure what to think about this, but failing a check ride is not a good thing, and in a unit, it could be devastating. When it was my turn, I went out with the examiner and, you guessed it, busted!

One day I went for another check ride, and there was another pilot who had recently arrived, a guy. He was due to have a check ride as well. I flew first and thankfully, I passed. The other officer was busted. I honestly felt that the examiner failed the male officer because he was the examiner who continued to fail the other woman officer. This way he could say he didn't fail only women! The other woman pilot who had arrived ahead of me was never successful as a pilot, and eventually went before a Flight Evaluation Board (FEB). An FEB is composed of rated aviator Army officers who are appointed to examine the qualifications of an officer for aviation service. The board reviews the officer's file to assess past performance, background, and qualifications, ultimately looking at the potential for continued aviation service. After a full review, the board makes recommendations to higher authorities. The role of the board is purely administrative; no recommendations for disciplinary actions are made. Essentially, the board's role is advisory in nature and not binding.[10] The FEB's recommendation for this officer was that she was unfit to be a pilot, essentially losing her wings. The recommendation of the board was accepted; she never flew again.

Although she stayed in the unit, worked for me, was a hard worker and frankly a fabulous officer who went on to have a very successful Army career, I didn't agree with the decision to keep her in the unit after taking her wings. This was a situation in which I believe the leadership did not do all they could have done for this young officer. I believe that once she started having trouble with the flight examiner, she probably should have been sent to another unit for a while to determine if she had an issue. For me, this was a fundamental failure of leadership and a lack of care and concern for another officer, another soldier, and fellow Army aviator. With some additional help and support, she would have passed her check rides and had a great career as an Army pilot.

My initial assignment in this unit was as the executive officer for, at the time, the largest aviation maintenance company of its kind in the Army. There were over three hundred soldiers assigned to the company. It was a good position, and I had the headquarters platoon, which consisted primarily of the administrative personnel.

I wanted the opportunity to lead one of the line platoons, specifically the UH-1 maintenance platoon. It took a while before I had

---

[10] Department of the Army (1 December 1983). Aviation Service of Rated Army Officers (AR 600-105). Washington, DC.

that opportunity. I spent a year as the executive officer and then was moved to primary staff where I became the battalion personnel officer, or an S-1. Basically, I led the human resources section.

I did like the position nonetheless. It allowed me to work closely with the battalion commander. However, I wanted a line platoon. After a year as an S-1, I was finally given the opportunity to lead the UH-1 maintenance platoon. I honestly believe that the battalion commander was reluctant to let a woman lead a line platoon, and for a couple of years he watched my performance as I served as the company executive officer and then as the battalion S-1. Eventually, I was given the opportunity.

Prior to taking over the platoon, I had a meeting with the company commander. I had worked for him previously as the executive officer. During the meeting I asked who my platoon sergeant, my right-hand man, would be. He told me the name, and I was shocked as I did not get along well with this particular NCO. Let's simply say we had had a couple of run-ins.

I said, "Sir, I can't believe you are assigning Sergeant First Class (SFC) Russell as my platoon sergeant!"

He replied, "Maureen, it will be fine."

The first day as the UH-1 platoon leader, I sat down with SFC Russell. After exchanging pleasantries, I said, "Let me tell you what I expect of my platoon sergeant."

I then proceeded to tick off my list of expectations, and upon finishing I asked, "Do you have any questions?"

He said, "No ma'am. I don't have any questions about what you expect of me as your platoon sergeant. However, can I now give you my expectations for you as my platoon leader?"

I have to admit, initially I was a bit surprised, but said, "Sure."

SFC Russell then said, "Ma'am I need you to be the heat shield between me and the company commander." Basically, he needed me to run interference.

"I can do that," I said.

We stood up and shook hands. I honestly don't know what happened, but in that moment, our relationship changed, and we became a team. We could not have been more different; however, I trusted him, and we got along well. While I had already been in the Army for a few years at that point, I still had a lot to learn, and he taught me a lot.

Chapter Four

MY ARMY JOURNEY – PART 2

Setting Standards

Leaders have to set the standard in the organization. When I was a young lieutenant, our post commander, a general officer, was not pleased with the amount of litter he would see on post. Each morning after formation, the soldiers would line up, walk along, and pick up debris in a well-known military activity referred to as 'police call.' One day the commanding general saw a cigarette butt, picked it up, wrote the date and put it back in the gutter. A week later the cigarette butt was still there. Needless to say, we all heard about that cigarette butt. However, it stuck with me, and I made sure the areas my unit was responsible for were always picked up and clean. Additionally, if I saw litter as I walked around post, I would pick it up. If you walk by something that is wrong, and don't make the correction, that becomes your new (lower) standard.

There is a lot of property and equipment in Army units. The leader has to sign for it and ultimately is responsible for the accountability and care of the equipment. I was in the process of conducting an inventory of all the property and equipment in the UH-1 maintenance platoon and came across several very large wooden boxes. Each had metal bands wrapped around them to keep them closed.

Stenciled on the outside was 'Maintenance Light Set 1 Each.' I asked one of the NCOs accompanying me if he would get something to cut the bands on the wooden boxes. I wanted to see the light sets. He did not want to open the box.

"Ma'am we know what is in there. Do you think it is necessary to cut the bands?" he asked.

"Yes, I want the bands cut. I'm signing for this property, and I'm going to see what I'm signing for," I responded.

He went to the tool room, returned with pliers, and proceeded to cut the bands. He lifted the lid and the box was empty, no light set. He proceeded to cut the bands on the other boxes – they too were empty. I didn't have to say a thing. New light sets were ordered and added to our property book.

Each week, we had another uniquely military activity called 'motor stables,' in which maintenance was performed on all of a unit's vehicles and equipment. The first week we had motor stables, I was walking around and noticed that our generators were lined up neatly out on the flight line but were not running. I asked one of the NCOs why the generators had not been turned on. He told me they checked the generators but didn't turn them on. I told the NCO that the generators needed to be checked and turned on each week. The next week when I was checking motor stables at the flight line, the generators were running; well, not all of them. Some of the generators did not work. It took a few weeks, but eventually all of the generators were humming as I walked the flight line during motor stables. The NCOs began to learn that I expected certain activities to be done routinely, and I walked around a lot.

The hanger we worked in was extremely old. In fact, it had been condemned, but we still worked in that building each day. It was an old facility and didn't always function well. One Saturday, we had to come in to work on some aircraft. It was midmorning, and all of the lights went off in the hanger. I said, "Let's get the generators out and set up the light sets." I didn't need to say anything about the inventory when I discovered the light sets were not in the boxes. Additionally, I didn't need to say anything about motor stables and getting all of our equipment operational. The NCOs and the soldiers knew.

SELECTED TO TEACH AT WEST POINT

Similar to how I was told I would never attend Flight School, I was also told by an Aviation Branch assignment officer that I would never go to West Point as a pilot and would never, ever go there as an instructor in the Department of Physical Education (DPE). However, once again, I went ahead and completed and submitted a packet for an appointment to DPE. In May 1983 while completing my final months of my three-year tour in Germany, I received a letter from DPE administrative officer informing me that Aviation Branch said I was not available until 1987. Interestingly, Aviation Branch didn't say I couldn't teach at West Point, only that I wasn't available for a few years. This was positive news.

When Joe and I returned to the states prior to traveling to our new assignments in Georgia, we stopped at USMA. Joe had already been selected to teach at West Point in the Department of Behavior Sciences and Leadership (BS&L) and was going to attend Georgia Tech to earn his master's degree while I was off to Forces Command in Atlanta to work as a staff officer. I had made an appointment to see the Director and Head of DPE. A lot of officers apply to teach in DPE each year, and it was a safe assumption that a meeting with the Director and Head of DPE to personally express my strong interest could very well give me an opportunity to stand apart from the rest. Prior to going into his office, I met with the Admin Officer. He was very helpful in prepping me for the meeting, advising me to stress my strengths and the different activities that I could teach. I walked into the meeting and almost as soon as I sat down, he said, "So Maureen, where do you want to go to graduate school?" In that moment I knew I was going to teach at DPE.

After the interview, Joe and I walked through the physical education building and I said, "Joe, I'm going to teach in DPE!" I didn't know when that was going to happen, however I was now confident that I would eventually teach at West Point.

A CHANGE IN PRIORITIES

During our time in Georgia, I became pregnant with our first child. His name is Joseph N. G. LeBoeuf, III. There are numerous Joes in the family: my husband, his dad, and two brothers-in-law. I wanted to make sure that when we said my son's name there was no confusion. My husband's family routinely called my husband Joe or Joey. There would not be a 'little Joe.' As we talked about a nickname, I recalled that my husband had a boss he liked and respected. His name was Jay. So, it was decided that our son would be called Jay.

I was a hard-charging young captain, and when I discovered I was pregnant, I decided I would continue to focus on the Army even after the baby was born. On July 7, 1984, that all changed. After twelve hours of labor and three and a half hours of pushing, our son arrived. He weighed a whopping 9 pounds, 10 ounces – a big baby. In that moment my world shifted. This little baby literally rocked my world. He was my new priority. The Army would no longer be number one.

JEALOUS?

In July 1984, a few days after Jay was born, my parents came for a visit. One evening as we sat down for dinner, the phone rang. It was my sister, Connie. She called to share the good news that she had been accepted as an intern at West Point in the Office of the Directorate of Intercollegiate Athletics. At the time, she was working on her master's degree in Sports Management at the University of Georgia. I couldn't believe she was going to be working at West Point. I cried, probably due to some postpartum depression, but also I was angry. Dad said, "I think you are jealous."

Jealous? You bet! I was jealous and infuriated. Going to West Point was what I wanted to do. Aviation Branch gave approval for me to teach in DPE but would not release me until 1987. It was still 1984. Joe was in grad school, and in June 1985 when he completed his studies, he would be headed to West Point. Me? With the current timeline, Joe and I would be separated for a few years. He would be leaving West Point at the time I would still be in graduate school. I wasn't sure what we would do.

A few weeks later, while I was still home on maternity leave, I received a call. I answered the phone, and the person on the other end said, "Maureen, it's Pat Oler." Pat and I had served together as staff officers in the 394th Transportation Battalion in Germany. He was the S3 Operations Officer. Every Friday night for at least a year, he and his wife, Jennifer, along with Joe and I, went to dinner at a local German *gasthaus*. He was a good friend and colleague. We had shared a lot of fun and challenging times in Germany. We exchanged some pleasantries and caught each other up on our families. I asked Pat, "What are you doing now?"

He said, "Maureen, I work at Aviation Branch in Personnel Command, and I'm your assignment officer." The assignment officer was the individual who decides my next assignment! Of course, it must meet the needs of the Army. Pat went on to say, "I was looking through your file and wondered if you are still interested in teaching in DPE." This was a big surprise; no, it was a HUGE surprise.

I probably stammered a bit, but spit out, "Yes, yes, I want to teach in DPE!" He said, "Maureen, we are going to make that happen." The month was August 1984. In March 1985, I was enrolled as a graduate student at the University of Georgia and a big step closer to teaching at DPE.

What changed? Did I become obstinate and bother my assignment officer weekly with my desire to get a master's degree and teach in DPE? No, but I did make sure that DPE knew that I was still interested. The people who make the personnel decisions in the Army change every few years, and those who said I would never teach at USMA had moved on. Things change, and it certainly helped to have a friend as my assignment officer. Relationships matter.

GRADUATE SCHOOL

Joe was finishing his master's degree when I was starting, and we had an infant. We decided it would be best if I rented an apartment in Athens, Georgia and stayed there Sunday through Thursday while Joe stayed with Jay during the week. It was not easy for Joe to have Jay all alone during the week, particularly having to get his master's thesis done in his last quarter. One evening Joe called and said, "Jay has the chicken pox." Needless to say, Joe missed a few days of class that week. If it were not for the assistance of several of his fellow graduate student colleagues and wonderful neighbors, he may not have completed his master's degree on time.

Nevertheless, Joe finished his degree that spring as expected, and in June 1985 he packed up and headed to West Point. Jay and I moved permanently into the little apartment in Athens. I was a geographical single parent for the next ten months.

I treated my days in graduate school as though I were in an Army unit. I was up at 4:40 a.m. each day, spending a few hours studying and getting ready for the day. I would wake Jay up and get him ready and then take him to day care, even if I didn't have class. At the end of the day, I would pick him up, and we would play, eat dinner, go through our bedtime routine – bath, read, brush, and pray. I would then spend several hours on schoolwork before I went to bed.

I worked extremely hard in graduate school. I did not have an undergraduate degree in physical education, so I had to take a number of additional courses. If the course ended in 'ology', I was taking it. Kinesiology, physiology, exercise physiology – you get the idea. At the end of each term, I had to send my grades to the Army. There was no way I was sending in a poor grade.

As a result of being a geographical single parent, I had to be disciplined around the rhythm of each day in order to stay on top of my homework and projects. On the first day of class, professors would review the syllabus and projects for the upcoming course. There were some professors who would say, "You will have a project, I'm not sure what it is yet." This was not helpful in my planning process.

When this happened, I would go up after class and say to the professor, "I need to know what our project is going to be as soon as possible." I knew that, being the sole caregiver for our son, my life would be unpredictable. I needed to get a jump on my work.

That summer was the first time we called on Birdie to help care for Jay. As mentioned earlier, Birdie came and spent several weeks with us which allowed me to focus on my schoolwork. Not to mention, of course, how wonderful it was to walk in at the end of the day and have dinner made.

At the beginning of the fall quarter, I had a huge amount of work, a lot of reading, reports and projects. It was overwhelming. One evening I was talking to Joe about this, and it was clear that I was stressed.

He said, "Mo, this is a big elephant, and you can only eat it one bite at a time. Write down all of your assignments and projects and when they are due on a sheet of paper. Post it somewhere in the apartment where it's visible. Then cross off each item once it's complete."

I did exactly that, wrote down each assignment on a piece of yellow, lined legal paper. It was taped on the wall near the kitchen. I remember vividly the day I crossed off the last assignment. It was a big elephant, and I did eat it one bite at a time.

It was not easy living in an apartment in a college town with a 1-year-old. We lived across the hall from three girls who attended UGA. Early one morning, it was 2:30 a.m., the music across the hall was so loud that it woke Jay and he started crying. This was a weeknight, not the weekend, and we both had to be up early. I opened my apartment door, and the door across the hall was wide open. The music was pulsing. I rang the bell and called out but got no response. Then I entered the apartment and eventually found one of the girls. I asked as politely as I could for them to please turn the music down. As I left their apartment, the door was slammed behind me and I heard her yell, "Bitch!"

I thought, *I hope you have triplets and live across the hall from drunk, loud college students.*

I have reflected on that experience, and to be honest, I didn't do anything to develop a relationship with those girls. It would have been easy for me to bake cookies and walk across the hall and introduce myself. No doubt that, because of the busyness of my life, I didn't think about it. Certainly, it would have been a better way to have my first encounter with my young neighbors.

Eventually my hard work paid off. I actually was selected for the Mary Ella Lunday Soule Scholarship. Mary Ella Lunday Soule was the Head of the Department of Physical Education for Women at the University of Georgia from 1925-1960. I received this award for

78

outstanding performance upon completion of the requirements for my master's degree. It was an unexpected recognition of hard work. Jay and I packed up our little apartment and headed north to join Joe at West Point.

THE DEPARTMENT OF PHYSICAL EDUCATION

Prior to arriving at West Point, I drove to Olean to visit my parents and take a few days' leave.[11] Late one morning the phone rang. It was my sponsor. A sponsor is someone in the organization that you are heading to who is assigned to communicate with you prior to your arrival. Additionally, they assist upon arrival to facilitate the transition, making it as smooth as possible. He said, "Maureen, where are you?"

I responded, "You called me, you know where I am." (This was before cell phones.)

He said, "You were supposed to be here two days ago."

I reminded him that he and I had had a conversation about my arrival date months earlier. There was a long pause on the other end of the line. He concluded with, "You need to be here tomorrow at 0600 for Cadet Basic Training (CBT)[12] physical training." He hung up.

I was in a panic! My parents' home was a six-hour drive to West Point, so at least I could get there as directed. I was glad my parents did not live in California. The big challenge was that Jay wasn't scheduled to begin daycare until the next week. Additionally, my new boss thought I was late arriving for my new job. This was a huge issue and not a good thing. I called Joe.

---

[11] Leave is time off in the military.

[12] Cadet Basic Training (CBT) is a six-week session for the new cadets when they first arrive at West Point.

Joe went over to DPE and spoke with the civilian faculty member who was in charge of CBT. He told Joe I could arrive at West Point on Monday morning and gave him the uniform I was to wear. I was relieved; it gave me a couple more days. However, I was concerned about the initial meeting with my new boss.

Joe met me at my parents' home that weekend and handed me my DPE uniform. Black shorts and a t-shirt with the DPE crest on the chest. I was thrilled to have my DPE uniform and ran upstairs to try it on. To my horror the shorts were very, very short. In high school I wore miniskirts, but this wasn't high school. I'm 5'9", in good shape and, yes, I have good legs; but the shorts were far too short for a captain in the U.S. Army, particularly of the female persuasion, to be wearing in front of cadets. Upon closer inspection, and to my deep, deep gratitude, the shorts had been hemmed, so I was able to let them down about two inches. Now at least I would look somewhat professional.

My first morning at West Point I met with the faculty member who had given me permission to arrive a few days later and had given Joe my uniform. He said, "If it isn't Captain LaLate!"

I smiled. Inside, I was seething.

Later that day I had an office call with my boss, the deputy of the department. He was a bear of a man, a two-sport athlete (wrestling and football) and an All-American as a cadet. As he sat at his desk, he had his hands clasped.

I remember thinking, *His forearms are huge!* I saluted and said, "Sir, Captain LeBoeuf reporting."

He returned the salute and said, "So, Captain, why did we think you were late reporting?"

I replied, "Sir, I believe there was some poor communication between my sponsor and me."

I had overlapped with my sponsor for a quarter while at UGA. Based on my observation of him in and out of the classroom, he was (to me) unimpressive. I honestly believe that the deputy knew that the poor communication was not on my part. My late arrival was never mentioned again.

My two years in DPE, from 1986 to 1988, passed quickly. I taught plebe[13] swimming, downhill skiing, self-defense, aerobic dance, running and wellness. During my first year, I was the Transportation and Building Officer. It was my responsibility to make sure that the transportation was scheduled for the classes that were too far for the cadets to walk to and when the cadets were bused to the ski slope in the winter. As the Building Officer, I was responsible for making sure all of the work orders were submitted and tracked.

My second year, I was the Administrative Officer. In my opinion, this is one of the best positions for an officer in the department. The Administrative Officer works directly for the Deputy of DPE and has close contact with the Director and Head of the Department of Physical Education, the Master of the Sword. It was in my position as Administrative Officer that I had the opportunity to see how the department was run, and I liked being close to the action.

The Department of Physical Education is a department that the cadets, with tongue-in-cheek, refer to as the *department with a heart*. It's a department with high standards, and if a cadet does not perform well physically, it's not a place they will want to go. Additionally, the military faculty selected to teach in DPE are all extremely physically fit and usually have some expertise and/or experience in certain sports; some have a world-class level of expertise. So, the faculty can be intimidating. A fellow captain had arrived the same time I did, and his office was across the hall from mine. He was a big man, an imposing figure and former captain of the Army football team.

---

[13] Plebe is the word used for a freshman at West Point.

The day we met he asked, "Are you related to Joe LeBoeuf?"

I said, "Yes, he is my husband."

He went on to tell me that when he was a plebe, Joe was a firstie in the same cadet company. A few weeks later, the officer and I were talking when Joe walked up. Joe is about 5'11" with a slight build. When he saw Joe, his entire demeanor changed. He actually came to the position of attention. Joe had not only been in the same company as this officer, he was also the regimental commander at the time, holding the highest leadership position in the regiment. In a plebe's life, the regimental commander would have been a big deal. This officer reverted back to his plebe self when he saw Joe. This was amazing for me to witness. I said, "Oh come on, relax." He laughed, but I'm not sure he was ever relaxed around Joe.

The majority of the officers who served in DPE were men, and their branches were in the combat arms[14]. During my second year, I worked very closely with an airborne, ranger, infantry officer. He was a nice guy, easy to work with, and he had a great sense of humor. He had never served with a woman.

After we had worked together for about six months, he said to me, "You are a pretty good officer."

I said, "The day we met I was a pretty good officer, it merely took you six months to realize it."

And yes, I have a wry sense of humor; it's a powerful survival technique. However, for me, it was an interesting comment. It certainly made me wonder how often other men had thought the same thing. My hope was that, because he had worked with me going forward, whenever he worked with a woman, he would expect that she would be a 'pretty good' soldier.

---

[14] Infantry, Armor, and Field Artillery are branches in which women at the time did not serve.

During the start of my second year at West Point, Joe and I were both selected to attend the Army's Command and General Staff College (CGSC) in Fort Leavenworth, Kansas. This was a 10-month course for mid-level officers or officers who had served approximately twelve years in the Army.

While in CGSC, I became pregnant. I had some issues following Jay's birth that were exacerbated during this pregnancy. During the last month or so of CGSC, the doctor wanted to place me on bed rest. I'm a good patient: I do what medical professionals ask of me. I promised the doctor that I would go to class, go home, and get into bed, which I did. Following the doctor's orders, I was able to successfully complete the last few weeks of CGSC.

FORT CARSON – 4ᵀᴴ INFANTRY DIVISION

We then moved to our next duty assignment, Fort Carson in Colorado. I knew that I had to go to the OB-GYN clinic, but I also had a house to settle. I did take it easy, and after a few days the house was in good shape, so I called the clinic and scheduled an appointment with the doctor who handled high-risk pregnancies.

I met the doctor, a fellow major in the U.S Army. We spoke for a few minutes about my pregnancy and what I was experiencing. He began his examination and stopped, and said, "I need to get the Chief of Obstetrics." He returned with the Chief who took a look, and then they talked to me about the possibility of being hospitalized for the remainder of my pregnancy. I asked if bed rest at home was an option and promised that I would do as requested. I was issued a wheelchair and placed on bed rest for the last three months of my pregnancy.

The next action I had to take was to call my new boss. My assignment was with the 4ᵗʰ Infantry Division's aviation brigade.

I called the brigade executive officer and said, "Sir, I have good news and bad news – seems to be the way it always is in life. The good news is that I am here, and the bad is that I have a high-risk pregnancy and have been placed on bed rest for the next three months."

His response was, "I'll have the brigade chaplain visit."

When I hung up, I thought, *I'm not sick. I'm pregnant.* I never heard from anyone in the aviation brigade again; not even the chaplain! At the time, my brother Timer and his wife, Sharon, had also been assigned to Fort Carson, and they lived across the street from us in Colorado Springs. When I told Sharon what happened she said, "I wonder how they would treat a male soldier who arrived and had a broken leg?"

Two weeks before my due date, I had an appointment with the doctor, who told me I had begun to dilate. This was great news, as I hadn't even had a contraction. I had often heard that the second delivery could be much easier than the first. The doctor sent me home and said to call him in the morning. Early the next morning I gave him a call, and he said to come on in. I still had not felt any contractions. Joe and I left for the hospital, I was admitted, and was settled into my room. The labor process was not progressing, so I was given Pitocin to help move it along. Finally, I was told I could begin pushing, and push I did for the next three hours.

The doctor came in and said, "Maureen you can push for another thirty minutes, and if the baby isn't born, I will perform a caesarean section (C-section.) Or, if you don't want to push anymore, we can do the C-section now."

He left the room so that Joe and I could discuss the C-section. The decision was made, and I had a C-section. Joe and I did not know the gender of the baby until she was born. Jackie arrived and quickly made her presence known with some very loud crying. She was healthy and weighed in at eight pounds. Interestingly enough, it never occurred to me the entire time I was on bed rest that I wouldn't have a full term, healthy baby.

Every OB-GYN I saw after I had Jay told me that I was done having children, and I needed to have a hysterectomy. After Jackie's birth, the doctor told me that if I got pregnant again, I would have to be on bed rest for the entire pregnancy, so three months after I delivered Jackie, I had the hysterectomy.

After some time to convalesce, I returned to work, but I wasn't sure that I wanted to continue to serve in the Army. Joe and I discussed this, and he said whether I stay or leave, he would support my decision. Resigning from the Army is not a quick process. I had to first submit a packet through my chain-of-command at Fort Carson, and then it was sent on to Personnel Command.

The year was 1990, the Army was downsizing, and they needed a lot of people to leave the profession -- hopefully more volunteers than forced departures. The submission of my packet would allow the Army to have one less person to downsize, but I was of a very small minority. I never received a phone call from my assignments officer asking why I had chosen to submit my resignation; there was no apparent interest nor concern. In hindsight, it is interesting that I was never contacted to possibly reconsider my decision. I believe I was one of two women officers in my year group who were aviators. Additionally, I had graduated from the CGSC, had a master's degree and a fairly strong military file. While I had willingly submitted my packet, it would have been nice to have been called and asked if this were something I wanted to do.

Joe and I attended a cocktail party, and I had an interesting conversation with one of the senior officers. He asked how I was doing, and I told him I was fine, and then I went on to say, "Sir, I'm getting out of the Army."

His response? "You can't leave the Army! The Army needs Maureen LeBoeuf!"

What a moment. I knew right then that I wanted to stay on active duty. In the car on the way home, I said to Joe, "I'm not going to leave the Army. I'm going to pull my packet back."

Because of the downsizing, it was not as easy to pull my packet back as I would have expected. Fortunately, my boss made a lot of phone calls, and eventually it happened. My resignation packet was returned to me without action. I was staying on active duty. This process allowed me to reflect on my commitment to the Army. I knew I both wanted and needed to stay there.

A few weeks later, a friend of Joe's called to tell him about a couple of Academy Professor positions opening up in the Department of Behavioral Sciences and Leadership (BSL), the department Joe had previously taught in at West Point. An Academy Professor is a non-rotating military position in which those assigned serve as senior members of the military faculty in the academic departments. Right before he hung up, he said, "And tell Maureen DPE will also be conducting a search for two Academy Professor positions." I can only imagine how I would have felt if I had recently gotten out of the Army.

Joe and I both applied for the positions and were both selected for an interview. In what was an incredibly low-probability event, we were also both selected by independent board processes for this unique opportunity. Clearly, someone was looking out for us. Our next assignment was a three-year graduate school contract to earn our doctorates as a prerequisite for joining the professional professoriate – as Academy Professors – at West Point. Joe headed to Georgia Tech, and I returned to the University of Georgia.

RETURN TO THE UNIVERSITY OF GEORGIA

We moved into a house in Athens, Georgia. We decided that one of us had to be close to the children in case of an emergency versus living halfway between Georgia Tech and UGA. I would get Jay and Jackie to school and daycare each day. Joe drove the one-and-a-half hour drive each way five days a week for two years to downtown Atlanta.

Graduate school can be an opportunity for more family time for some families. For us, this was definitely not the case. Joe would get up and leave early and would return home around dinnertime or later, all in order to avoid the Atlanta traffic, which would often turn a 90-minute drive into a 2½-hour drive – not fun! It was especially challenging for both of us to be working on our doctorates simultaneously. Earning a doctorate is hard work and has a political nature to it as well.

My major advisor, a woman with whom I worked during my previous time at UGA, was a tough taskmaster and had been the department chair. There were some in the department who didn't care much for her. A major hurdle when working on a doctorate is being accepted into candidacy. This is accomplished after a specific amount of coursework is completed, and then after a sufficient period of study and preparation, one sits for preliminary exams, takes an oral exam with members of the committee, and has the first three chapters of their dissertation written. Normally, it took two years to arrive at this point in the UGA Physical Education Department.

Having started my doctoral studies in August 1991, I met with my major advisor in January 1992. She told me that she wanted me to sit for my exams in May. Not May 1993, which would have been the norm. No, not for me, too easy! She wanted me to sit in five months. I asked about the timing, and she assured me I would be fine. Part of her reasoning was that she was going to retire prior to the date of my scheduled graduation date, June 1994. However, if I sat for my exams and passed, I could petition the Dean and request that she remain as my major professor, even though she would have formally retired.

She was concerned that if I were not admitted into candidacy, some faculty members might make it difficult for me to graduate on schedule. I honestly believe this was an unwarranted concern because I was an excellent student and felt well-respected by the faculty. I agreed to move forward with the accelerated plan. I did not share this new guidance and directive with any other doctoral candidates because I felt it would have caused a bit of an uproar.

The day I sat for my exams, my husband saw a classmate of mine who was a retired Army officer and interestingly, my former boss when I taught in DPE. He asked where I was, and Joe told him I was sitting for my exams. He became quite angry that I had been allowed to move so quickly through the candidacy process. He was ahead of me in the program. Joe told him that this was not my idea and that I was doing as my major advisor had asked. While most of the time my fellow students were fine, sometimes they could be a challenge.

There was a woman ahead of me in the program who considered herself the fair-haired girl and the major advisor's favorite student. Then I arrived at UGA and had the same major advisor. Apparently, she grew concerned that I had replaced her as the favorite. I remember thinking, *What are we twelve? Are we back in middle school?* Ah, the challenges of a graduate program. It is not only about academics.

I sat for my preliminary exams and then went through the oral exam, passed and was admitted to candidacy. A big hurdle that occurred much sooner than I expected, I was now a doctoral candidate. Work on my doctoral studies continued for the next two years. Life was busy with two young children and both of us working on our doctorates.

In June 1994, I received my Doctorate of Education from the University of Georgia. It was a significant achievement for me, a joyful time for our family, and Mom and Dad were present for my graduation. I'm sure that of all the children in my family, I am not the one Mom would have thought would ever have accomplished this level of academic achievement. I always say that Ph.D. stands for perseverance, hard work, and dedication. Or, as some would say, piled higher and deeper. Nevertheless, I had earned the credential that would enable my continued work at West Point as a permanent member of the faculty, an Academy Professor.

BEING A WOMAN IN THE ARMY

I can't write about my experiences in the Army without addressing the issue of sexual harassment. I came on active duty in July 1976. At the end of that fiscal year, which is September, there were a total of 49,500 women in the Army, and 5,100 were officers.[15] The percentage of women in the military, officers and enlisted combined, was approximately six percent, and women officers made up about half of one percent. I knew there were not a lot of women officers in the Army; however, I had no idea there were so few.

I always felt very fortunate in working with men; I honestly had very few problems. The first time I was a platoon leader, I had eighty-five men assigned to the platoon, no women. There were times when I could actually feel if a guy didn't think I belonged. I could tell by the way he responded to me.

I did have a few situations in dealing with men over the years that would be considered harassment. One day I was walking through my platoon's area at the port, and someone whistled a big wolf whistle.

---

[15] http://www.history.army.mil/books/DAHSUM/1976/ch05.htm, accessed February 23, 2016.

What did I do? Nothing. I didn't look around, didn't respond, and simply kept walking. It never happened again.

Occasionally we would leave Fort Eustis and go to the field for a training exercise. On one particular instance, we settled into an area, with tents up and vehicles parked, where we would spend the next few weeks. I was walking around checking the status of the site when two of my soldiers came running up to me and said, "Hey Lieutenant, look what we found!"

Then one of the soldiers pulled something from behind his back. It was a large, black snake, and fortunately it was dead. Now, it's fair to say I have a healthy dislike of snakes, dead or alive. However, in that moment I knew it would not be a good idea to react. So, in spite of my personal feelings of anxiety I looked at the snake and said, "Cool!"

They walked off obviously disappointed that I didn't react as they had hoped. A few days later I saw one of the soldiers running through the woods, obviously scared. I found out he was running because he saw a snake! Sometimes it's a good thing for a leader not to react.

When stationed in Germany, I was conducting a pre-flight inspection on an aircraft prior to a flight. The pilot is usually escorted by the crew chief, and together they make sure the aircraft is air worthy. On that day the crew chief was a sergeant (E5.) We were under the aircraft taking a fuel sample when the crew chief began asking me about my plans for the weekend. Thinking this was simply casual conversation, I told him I didn't have any big plans. He then asked me out on a date. My initial reaction was shock. I was dating Joe (although he was still in the states), and I wondered if I had given this sergeant some type of signal that I was interested and available. I quickly dismissed that thought because I was always very professional.

I asked him, "Sergeant, are you asking me out?"

He responded in the affirmative.

I said, "Sergeant, I don't fraternize with enlisted soldiers."

Without hesitation he said, "According to Army regulations it's not fraternization if I don't work directly for you."

I thought, *Oh my goodness, he has actually researched this*. Once again, I said, "Sergeant, I don't fraternize with enlisted soldiers." It never happened again!

Another incident occurred when I was a major stationed in the 4th Infantry Division with the aviation brigade. I had over twelve years in the Army by this point. One day I was walking down the hall to a weekly command and staff meeting with our brigade commander. The commander of the Apache battalion (the Apache is the Army's primary attack helicopter), a lieutenant colonel, walked up behind me and squeezed my hair that was pulled back in a bun. He said, "Nice bun!"

In that moment I knew he wasn't referring to my hair. I felt this horrible feeling in the pit of my stomach. A half-dozen or so thoughts raced through my head: *Should I tell the brigade commander? There are no women in his unit. I'm a major, I can handle this!*

I immediately changed my behavior around this individual. If he came into my office, I always stood up and would not allow him to close the door. If there were social functions and he was drinking, I always gave him a wide berth. I never told anyone about this, not even my husband. I departed the unit at the end of my tour.

One afternoon while attending the University of Georgia pursuing my doctorate, the phone rang, and I answered. On the other end of the line was an Army lawyer. He was calling from the 4th Infantry Division.

He said, "Ma'am, I'm calling to talk to you about Lieutenant Colonel X." As soon as he said his name, the aforementioned *Nice bun!* incident came to mind.

The lawyer went on to say, "Did he ever do anything that you would have considered sexual harassment?"

I shared my story, and he responded, "Ma'am, that was not sexual harassment. He touched you, so technically that was assault!"

The lawyer told me that a woman had come forward with a complaint about this individual, and subsequently, others had as well. As part of the investigation, women who had been in the aviation brigade with the individual in question were being called. He told me that the next day a major general, the investigating officer, would call me, swear me in, and I would tell my story, which I did. As a result of the investigation, the officer was forced to retire.

One day as I was walking across campus at UGA, I thought I saw him. The feeling of panic was overwhelming. It was not him; however, for several weeks after, I would look for him thinking, *What if he came after me?*

Upon reflection, I did not handle this situation well when it first happened. I try not to beat myself up over this. However, I should have gone immediately to my brigade commander. He would have listened to me and would have counseled the officer. If I had addressed it immediately, possibly others would not have been subjected to his inappropriate comments and behavior. Learning the power of having the courage to 'get it right' and not merely 'get along' was an important emerging lesson from this experience.

CHAPTER FIVE

LEADING ON THE HOME FRONT

DAD

Dad was a patriarch in every sense of the word. Dad was strict in his behavior, with very high standards and expectations. In seventh grade, we moved from Barry Street to Fulton Street, which was only a few blocks away, and the 'Emergency Route' was changed. Now we could simply walk to the corner of Fulton Street and head straight down Henley Street to St. Mary's.

Mom and Dad had been looking for a bigger home in Olean. There was one particular house that they submitted a bid on, and under the cover of darkness, some of us went with mom to the house and buried a statue of Saint Joseph in the lawn. You see, Saint Joseph is the patron saint of buying or selling a house. We didn't get that house. When we looked at the house on Fulton Street, Mom and Dad took several of us girls dressed in our 'sister dresses.' This tactic was used because the owner had several daughters. Lo and behold, the Fulton Street owners accepted our parents' offer! The sister dresses had done the trick.

Compared to the house on Barry Street, the house on Fulton Street was quite large and pretty spectacular. There were hardwood floors throughout. The woodwork was not painted, and it was all tiger oak. There were chandeliers in several of the rooms downstairs, and there were several sets of large pocket doors. There were three living rooms, a formal dining room, a study, five bedrooms, one full bathroom, a bathroom with a sink and shower, a powder room, and an attic where the boys slept. I no longer shared a bedroom with three sisters. I only had one roommate in this new house, Dee Dee.

On the slate roof there were four chimneystacks, and there were eight marble fireplaces in the house, yes eight! There was one fireplace in each of the three living rooms, in the dining room, and in each of the four bedrooms on the second floor. Each fireplace had a mantle, pillars, and a large mirror. Colorful tiles surrounded the fireplaces. They were gorgeous.

The house on Fulton Street was a big, wonderful house. When we moved in, we were told that we would have to keep the bedrooms picked up and clean. To make sure the rooms met Dad's standards, he had an inspection. We all had to stand by and wait for him to come to our rooms. As you can see, I was trained for the military very early in my life. Dee Dee and I worked hard to clean our room, and we were ready, or so we thought. Dad walked into the room, reached up, and ran his hand along the top of the mantle. He brought down his hand and showed us dust. The inspection was over. As he left the room he said, "Let me know when your room is ready to be inspected."

While Dad had high standards, he also had a caring, thoughtful side. My dad was a note and letter writer. I received a letter in the mail from Dad when I had been accepted at St. Bonaventure. It didn't matter that it was the only school to which I had applied. Writing a letter of congratulations was Dad's way of letting me know that college was an important step in my life.

When I went into the Army for my initial twelve-week training program, Dad wrote me a letter each day. He told me that if I had been home, he would talk to me each day, so he wrote a daily letter.

Dad also knew that getting mail in the military was important. Each day we would have mail call. We would stand in formation, and the names of those who received mail would be called out. I received mail almost every day.

A fellow platoon member asked me who was writing to me. I told her that it was my dad. She said, "My parents would never write to me."

One day she came into my room and said, "Can I read one of the letters your dad wrote?" She read the letter and said, "You are so lucky."

There were several other times during our time together when she would come into my room and ask to read one of the letters from Dad. Yes, I was lucky.

About four weeks into flight school, I had a classmate commit suicide. It was both devastating and unnerving. He was a graduate of the United States Air Force Academy (USAFA) and very smart; in fact, he was already at the top of our class. Several of us socialized together, and he was in the group. I had arranged to get some notes from him, and one evening I walked over to his Bachelor Officer's Quarters (BOQ). It was around dinnertime, and I was struck by a couple of things. His table was neatly set for dinner – a place setting with knife, fork and spoon and a folded napkin. I also noticed a bookshelf in his room and almost every book was spiritual in nature. He even had a cross on the stone of his USAFA class ring. He was a deeply spiritual and fundamentally nice guy.

One Friday evening we were gathering at a friend's apartment for a party. I knew he was invited and asked where he was. The girl who was hosting said that he had called and wasn't able to attend. The following Monday morning we had a test and he wasn't in class. I asked the person who was his best friend, another USAFA grad, if he had seen him. He said he hadn't seen him all weekend, but his car was in the parking lot. We went to a fast-food restaurant for a bite to eat after the test. As I drove into the parking lot in front of my BOQ, I saw a lot of military police cars and personnel at the BOQ next to mine. It was his BOQ building, and I knew he was dead. He had confided with a classmate that he was contemplating suicide.

I called home and talked to Mom and Dad. The following is the letter my dad wrote to me:

```
                                               Wed. 26th Sept.

Dear Mo:
              I had trouble falling asleep last night
because I was mulling over our conversation. I concluded that the
business of parenting is not what it is advertised to be. When we
try to help  our children with problems we most often fail.
              In the light of morning I still do not know
what I could have said that would have made you feel any better. Even
now all I can say is that these things do happen in life. And the
everlasting "Why?" remains shrouded in mystery. When a person dies
that way, especially one so young, it seems such a waste. And, I
know, each person who knew him has to wonder if there was anything
that he could have done, or should have done, which might have
prevented it.
              This is one of those instances in which one
has to accept the fact that it happened, and that, in some way we do
not understand, it was God's will. For me, at least, that is an
answer I can live with.
              On a happier note: the day before yesterday
my golfers beat Jamestown and gave me my 100th win. It was a long
time coming, and after the qualifying rounds in early September I
told Mom that there was simply no way I could win even one match. Yes,
they are that weak. But apparently, this is a poor year for golfers becau
other coaches tell me they feel the same way. The level of golf is
markedly above average this year. All I can say is that my beaters are
not quite as bad as some of the others they have met.
              I began coaching in '68, and my record to
date is 100-70 and 9. So, I guess that isn't too bad, although I am
not at all sure how much credit I can claim. I guess, in the final
analysis, !I'm the man who drives the bus!"
              I keep meaning to get my E-6B computer out to
have a look at it. I am sure I will not recall too much about its
operation.But that does remind me of something I wanted to suggest to
you.
              I always worked very hard to develop my
awareness of direction, both day and night. Standing on the ramp before
takeoff, driving in a car, even walking around the base: I always
was aware of north. I still am, and to tell the truth, I rather enjoy
that. In addition, always think in terms of reciprocals so that, if
need be, you can turn around and start to retrace your course without
at first referring to your compass. In a sense, I carry a compass rose in
my mind . . .always. Of course, the compass itself does come in handy
at times. Enough of that.
              Tonight Mom, Sharon, Timer and I come out to
school to see Showboat. The lead is to be played by Forrets Tucker
that is Forrest Tucker. He played the Sgt. on F. Troop. In addition,
Butterfly McQueen is in it. If you saw Gone With the Wind you might
remember her as the young black girl who claimed she knew how to
act as a midwife, but when Scarlett was about to have the baby burst
into tears." I don't know nuthin' about birthin' a baby," was her
line.
              Enough. Time to run to the P.O. to get this
off to you. Hopefully it will arrive Saturday.
                                            Love,  Dad
```

Dad wrote often, and usually there were words of encouragement, the weather, family news and always, *Love, Dad.* The letter he wrote after the suicide was exactly that type of letter.

One summer I was home on leave and talking to Dad about the public speaking course he was going to be teaching during the academic year. I went on to ask if he included PowerPoint as a part of his course. He asked, "What is PowerPoint?"

I offered to go to St. Bonaventure and teach a lesson to his class on PowerPoint. We agreed on a date in October during the first semester. It was in a tiered classroom and right before class began, Mom silently entered the room from a back door and took a seat. I was in uniform, and we decided it would be less distracting if I was not introduced as his daughter. Dad introduced me as a former student, which was true. I enjoyed teaching the class, and I know Dad was learning how to effectively use PowerPoint as well. Upon the conclusion of the class, I thanked the students and Professor Keenan. I did say, "Oh, by the way, Professor Keenan is my dad."

I returned to West Point, and a few days later, a note arrived in the mail from Dad. It was written in his recognizable penmanship with one of his treasured fountain pens. It was a lovely note of thanks. Of course, Dad had thanked me after I taught the class and again later as I was getting ready to depart. The hand-written note was to let me know how truly special it had been for him to have me teach his class. Here is that note.

Leo E. Keenan, Jr.

10/24/2000

Dear Mo:

Your generosity in giving your time, talent and expertise in my behalf is something I will not soon forget.

At Sea I had the joy of watching you land a helicopter at Fort Rucker I never dreamed that one day you would return to Bona's to instruct my classes.

Your lecture was such that I learned something each time I heard it. And I know the students (at least most of them!) enjoyed having you.

Please accept my sincere thanks.

Love,
Dad

During my Army career I became emotional in front of my boss three times, and interestingly enough, each time it was the Commandant of Cadets at the United States Military Academy when I was a colonel. One of those times was after my dad died. I had returned to work after the funeral; the commandant asked me if I was okay, and I said yes, but I wasn't.

THE LOSS OF MY DAD

I believe the loss of a parent at any age is profound. In December 2001, there were reports from home that Dad was not feeling well. He had a few trips to the doctor and a brief stay at the hospital. Joe and I had planned a vacation with the kids to Hawaii for the Christmas holiday. On Christmas day, I called home. My mom said that Dad had stayed in bed all day and hadn't even opened his gifts. I began to wonder if he was sicker than we all knew. A few of my brothers and sisters had visited Dad. A couple of weeks after Christmas, one my sisters sent a picture on the computer through e-mail of Dad sitting in his chair. The way the picture came through, it loaded very slowly from the top to the bottom. As the picture loaded and I saw Dad's eyes, he did look sick to me.

On January 20, my best friend called. She is the head dietician at the local hospital and had gone by the house to visit Dad.

We exchanged some pleasantries, and then she said, "Mo, when do you plan to come home?" I told her I would be going home over spring break.

She said, "Mo, you need to come home sooner rather than later."

I said, "What are you telling me?"

Her response, "Mo, your dad is dying."

I felt like I had been kicked in the gut. Joe and I decided that we would go home later in the week.

Early on the morning of January 25th, the day we were heading home, I checked my e-mail to discover that during the night Dad was taken via ambulance to the hospital. A proud man, he walked to the ambulance. Joe, Jackie and I drove to Olean later that day. As we walked into his hospital room, Dad smiled. Mom was there along

99

with my sister, Birdie. I kissed Dad and thought he looked okay. We then chatted for a bit.

I had given a talk earlier in the week, and because Dad taught public speaking at St. Bonaventure and he gave lots of talks himself, whenever I gave a talk, Dad wanted to hear all about it. There were always many questions from Dad: Where was the talk? How many people? What was the talk about? What jokes did you tell? Did they laugh?

I said, "Dad, I gave a talk this week."

He said, "That's nice."

Not a single question about the talk? This was so unlike my Dad, and in that moment, I knew he was quite sick. After being there for a very short visit, Dad told us we could leave. Again, very unlike Dad. We left and went to Pizza Hut to get dinner to take to the house. As we waited for the pizza, I sat there and cried.

The next day I got up early. Mom and I went to the hospital. Once again, Birdie was there. As we walked in, she said, "Dad has a fever." I knew that was not good. Birdie left the hospital since she had something to do with her girls. Mom and I sat with Dad, and it was quite clear that he was very uncomfortable. During the morning I felt that we needed to call a priest to administer the Sacrament of the Sick. I asked Mom if that would be okay, and she agreed.

When you are one of a large family, it is important to keep others informed. Of course, with my military background, I thought that I needed to let my oldest brother, Timer, know that I was going to call a priest. He said, "Mo, you are on the ground and have situational awareness. If you think you need to call a priest, make the call." Timer is a retired United States Army Colonel.

First, I called the rectory at St. Mary's. My parents were parishioners at St. Mary's for decades. There was no answer, and I left a voice mail. I then called the friary at St. Bonaventure, where Dad had recently completed his 52nd year as a member of the faculty. Again, no answer. I left a voice mail. I couldn't believe how difficult it was to locate a priest in a small city with five Catholic parishes and a Catholic university. Eventually, a priest came into the room. I introduced mom and myself. It was obvious that mom did not know this priest.

She said to him, "This is Leo Keenan, do you know him?"

He responded, "No." In this moment when Dad was to receive the Sacrament of the Sick, the priest administering this sacrament didn't know Dad.

My brothers and sisters who lived out of town began calling during the day. When they asked if they should come home, I replied, "Yes."

Timer lived in Virginia and had been home the previous weekend. Kathy lived in Olean. Judie lived in Rochester and came home. Bob lived locally. Dee Dee lived in Boston and also had been home the previous weekend. Connie lived in Japan. Timer called her and told her to come home. Birdie lived locally, and Kevin, who lived in Buffalo, also came home.

Around lunchtime, Mom and I went to the cafeteria for a bite to eat. As we sat there, Mom said, "I don't know when we got old." Mom was so sad. This was such a painful comment for me to hear.

Dad was in a semi-private room. As the others started to arrive, the room was getting crowded. Each time the nurse came into the room she came to me. I was wearing a red sweater-set and wondered if that was the reason.

At one point she came to me and said, "We are going to move your Dad to a private room and bring in a comfort cart."

I said, "Thank you. What is a comfort cart?" She said it would have juices, crackers and cookies for the family. I thought that was nice.

During the afternoon, Mom asked me if I would go to the house and pick up a couple of items. While I was home, the phone rang; it was my aunt calling. She had been married to Dad's younger brother. I told her that Dad was in the hospital; she didn't know. She said that her daughter was in Ellicottville skiing, and if we needed to talk, she would be glad to come down. Her daughter owned nursing homes and had a lot of knowledge about health care and the elderly. Without hesitation, I asked my aunt to have her come to Olean. I gave her a time and told her to meet us at the house. Now I was setting up a meeting without asking anyone.

I went back to the hospital and told everyone that we were to meet our cousin at our family home around 6:00 p.m. My best friend, Mary, who worked at the hospital, stayed with Dad. We sat with our cousin, and she asked a lot of questions about Dad and what was going on. At one point I mentioned the private room and the comfort cart. She indicated that when they bring in the comfort cart, the patient is probably dying. She also said that we could ask for comfort measures. No poking and prodding, no more blood draws, just make Dad comfortable.

We went back to the hospital, and she asked if she could come with us. A nurse came into the room and took Dad's blood pressure. My cousin asked what his blood pressure was, but the nurse wouldn't tell her. She asked again, no response. The nurse left the room. There was no clear reason for the nurse not to respond, but the probable reason was that Dad's blood pressure was very, very low.

Earlier in the day someone handed me a small blue book. The title was *Gone from My Sight: The Dying Experience*, written by Barbara Karnes, a registered nurse who worked extensively in hospice care. This little book explained what to expect when someone is dying. As I read the book, I realized that Dad was going through all of the various stages discussed in the book, and he was very close to death. It was a Saturday night. Judie and Bob said they would spend the night with Dad.

I couldn't sleep, so at about 5:00 a.m. the next day I got up and headed to the hospital. I honestly thought that Dad would die that night. When I walked in, Judie said it had been a restless night. Lots of picking at his sheets, talking to people who were not in the room, and Dad even asked for a martini, his favorite drink!

I spent some time at the hospital and right before I left, I said, "Dad, I love you."

He said, "I love you, too."

It was Sunday, and we needed to get Jackie back to West Point for school. I stood in the kitchen talking with Judie, debating on whether I should stay or go. I knew Dad was going to pass soon. I decided to go back to West Point because I had a lot to do before I returned home for Dad's funeral. The drive from Olean to West Point was about six hours. Shortly before we arrived at West Point, I received a missed call from my oldest brother. I called Timer, and he said, "Dad passed away at 2:30 p.m."

My dad was gone, and I was devastated.

Fortunately, after the funeral, I was able to get away for a few days. During that time, I was scheduled to speak at the University of Richmond's Army ROTC Military Ball, where my niece was a cadet. After my introduction at the start of my talks I would normally say, "Now that's an introduction that my dad would be proud of, and Mom would actually believe." That night, 'would be proud' turned into 'would have been proud.' I used the past tense because Dad was gone. I locked eyes with my niece at that moment and thought I would lose it. Fortunately, I didn't and finished my talk.

JACKIE'S STORY

The senior year of high school was an exciting time for my daughter, Jackie. It was full of the usual high-school activities, dances, dating, playing lacrosse, and of course thinking about the next phase of her life, going off to college.

In addition to my dad graduating from and teaching at St. Bonaventure for 52 years, my eight brothers and sisters and I are all Bonas graduates, and six nieces and nephews are Bonas graduates as well. I also served for nine years as a Trustee at Bonas, so I consider us to be a St. Bonaventure University legacy family.

Jackie never expressed any interest in Bonas, however. When she began looking at colleges, I asked her to at least visit Bonas. I told her she didn't have to apply, but I wanted her to take a look. She was convinced that because she had been on campus countless times with her grandfather and me, she knew all there was to know about the university. I told her that while she had been around Bonas for years, she had never looked at it through the eyes of a potential student, so she agreed to accompany me to campus when I next traveled there to attend a Board meeting. It was a cold, snowy day in March. Jackie met her tour guide, attended class with a cousin, and then met the daughter of a fellow Trustee for lunch. She and I met later in the day.

I asked Jackie about her visit, and to my surprise, she actually liked Bonas. She was especially impressed with how much her guide actually knew about the university. A few weeks later she told me she wanted to attend college there. I was both surprised and thrilled. Our son had graduated from USMA, Joe's alma mater, and now Jackie would attend mine. She would be the seventh of her generation to go to St. Bonaventure.

Since she decided that she wanted to go to Bonas, she did not apply to any other schools. We had talked about this, but Jackie was adamant the she did not want to go to school in North Carolina where we were living at the time, and that Bonas was the place for her. She applied in early November, received her acceptance, and we mailed in her deposit. I had heard friends talk about the stress of the college application process. In fact, I have a niece who visited nine colleges and applied to seven. What we experienced was easy. It was so exciting. I sent an e-mail to the family and my fellow Board members about Jackie's acceptance and how she would be a member of the class of 2012.

Jackie's second semester of her senior year of high school flew by. She played lacrosse on her high school team. She was one of the team captains, was named MVP, was selected to participate in the North Carolina East-West All Star Game, and she was selected and played in the 2008 Girls North Carolina State Games where her team won the gold medal. Particularly for Jackie, it was a great way for her to finish her high school years and build some incredibly powerful memories.

Summer arrived, and we had a couple of trips planned along with getting Jackie ready for college. We traveled to St. Bonaventure in July to attend one of the orientation sessions and stayed in the hotel across the street from the university. The first morning of the orientation as I went to my car, I saw a woman getting into a car parked next to mine. I asked her if she was the parent of future Bonaventure student. She said yes, and I told her I was as well. She also had a daughter and told me her daughter was quite nervous. I responded that my daughter was nervous as well.

Once checked in, Joe and I walked Jackie up to her dorm room where she was to spend the night. To my surprise, we walked in and there stood the woman I had talked with in the parking lot earlier. Our daughters would be roommates for the night. I said, "This will always be the very first person you met here at St. Bonaventure." I think Jackie might have rolled her eyes.

It was fascinating for me to go through this orientation as a parent. It was done so very well. Joe was equally impressed, and he enjoyed getting to know St. Bonaventure. He too had been on campus numerous times but never actually walked around and learned about the history of the university. That evening we attended a service in the chapel. Twenty-six years earlier on that same day, Joe and I were married there.

The tagline at St. Bonaventure was "*Becoming extraordinary*." The orientation focused on how the students will become extraordinary during their four years at Bonas. Jackie seemed to enjoy the orientation and especially liked her roommate, Sarah. Through Facebook and texting, they kept in touch over the remainder of the summer.

Returning back to North Carolina, the final weeks before Jackie's departure were spent shopping with checklist in hand and purchasing all of those 'must have' items. It was fairly easy because Jackie didn't seem to care too much about what color and type of bedding we purchased. In fact, I was out and called her about something I saw, and she said to go ahead and get it, she didn't care. This was a bit of a surprise to me because Jackie has always been very opinionated about her room and the way it looked. At the time I didn't give this too much thought.

There were times during the summer when we would talk about going off to college. I would ask if she had any concerns. The only concern she ever mentioned was being homesick. I always replied, "Everyone gets homesick."

The day arrived when Jackie and I were to drive to St. Bonaventure. With the car packed, we headed north. It is a 600-mile drive from our home in North Carolina to St. Bonaventure, and the trip was uneventful. We spent the night with my sister Kathy and her husband. The next day Katie, a cousin, arrived from Concord, Massachusetts, with her mom, Dee Dee. Dee Dee arranged for her daughter to pick up her room key a day early so that she could get her items into her room. Katie took Jackie with her, and she too got her room key early.

This was great for us. We were going to miss the hectic day of moving in with the other 544 members of the freshman class. Within a couple of hours everything was moved into Jackie's room and set up, ready for effective college living. Easy!

Joe flew up the next day and was surprised to find all the heavy lifting done. We enjoyed a beautiful day at Bonas. Jackie texted Sarah (her roommate from orientation), and we went over to visit for a while with her family. Then we went to Jackie's room and had a chance to meet her roommate. Another Sarah, she was a very nice girl from a dairy farm a few hours east of St. Bonaventure. We had dinner at my sister's house that evening, and Jackie returned to campus for a floor meeting at 7:30 p.m.

Later that night there was a candlelight ceremony for the Class of 2012. It was dark, and the families lined a walkway leading up to Plassman Hall, an academic building. The students walked silently up the walkway, which was lined with luminarias, and stood at the base of the steps. Sister Margaret Carney, the President of the University, along with several members of her cabinet, led the ceremony.

There was an invocation; a welcome from Sr. Margaret; a reminder from the Provost, Dr. Mike Fischer, to study; a letter read from the Class of 2008; lighting of the candles; the class pledge; Prayer of St. Francis; the singing of the Alma Mater; and a recessional. It was a perfect ending to the day and a perfect beginning for Jackie's journey at this very special place.

We linked up with Jackie after the ceremony and walked her to her dorm. She had tears in her eyes, but she was not crying. I did not cry. I felt so good about Jackie being at my beloved St. Bonaventure. She was where I felt in my heart that she needed to be. At St. Bonaventure she would become extraordinary!

Joe drove to the Buffalo airport and flew back home, and I began the 600-mile drive. Over the next couple of days, we received text messages from Jackie and some phone calls. She was homesick. Being homesick is normal.

"Stay busy, meet people, it will get easier," was our consistent advice over the next few days. I even Googled 'homesickness' and was pleased to discover that everything we were telling Jackie to do was on the mark. Also, Joe has a doctorate in psychology, so we were confident that we were doing and saying the right things.

The Monday after I returned from New York, I spent at least two hours on the phone with Jackie. Joe spent as much if not more time talking with her. In between calls were the non-stop text messages.

"I'm homesick!"

"I don't think I can do this!"

I had to give a speech on Tuesday evening and asked Jackie to not call on Tuesday so that I could focus on the talk. I only received a couple of text messages and no calls. I gave my speech that evening, but upon my return home the phone rang, and it was Joe. He had spent an hour and 45 minutes on the phone with Jackie. It wasn't getting better, in fact it was worse.

After I spoke with Joe the phone rang again. It was Jackie, and she begged me to let her come home. I offered to come up to Bonas instead, and the next morning, I called the Counseling Center at Bonas. I spoke with a counselor and told her about Jackie. The counselor told me she would clear her afternoon calendar so that Jackie could see her. I talked with Jackie and told her she must go to the counseling center. However, Jackie continued to press me to come back to Bonas.

This is the e-mail I sent to the counselor...

Thank you so very much for your time this morning. Jackie is a mess today, wants to come home. I just spoke with her and told her that she is to call you and see you this afternoon. She has a class until 2:20, I told her to be at your office at 2:25.

Thanks,

Maureen

I spoke with Jackie after the counseling session, and she said it seemed to help. However, she still wanted me to come up. On Thursday, six days after I returned home from Bonas, I once again made the 600-mile trip north. As I approached the university, I called Jackie and made plans to meet her at my sister's house. An hour later she arrived with her cousin, Katie. Jackie and I hugged and then went to be alone so that we could talk. As soon as I saw her, I could see how unhappy she was. I decided to stay in Olean for a week, having no doubt that the situation would improve by the end of my visit. I saw Jackie every day, but I made sure that it wasn't until later in the day.

By the end of that week, Jackie thought she would be okay after I left. Joe and I would be back mid-September for Family Weekend, and I would return again for a Board meeting the first week of October. Jackie then would be flying home for mid-semester break on October 10. We would deal with the weeks between fall break and Thanksgiving later. We had a plan.

I received several texts during my trip back home and they seemed good, most were only checking on my driving progress. The next few days went along okay. Jackie was still calling and texting, but not quite as much. Also, I had told her that although I understood that she was homesick, I didn't want her homesickness to be the focus of our calls.

On Wednesday she called and said that Aunt Judie mentioned, "It was too bad that she had classes on Friday, otherwise she could go with her to Ohio."

Judie's daughter was a sophomore at Duke University, and she played soccer. The team had two games in Ohio over the weekend. Judie, Kathy, and my brother, Kevin, were driving to the games. On Wednesday when Jackie went to class, all of her Friday classes had been cancelled. I did not want her to go to Ohio. I thought she should learn how to entertain herself and not rely on her aunts. However, she wanted to go, so Joe and I agreed that she could go. I called Judie, to tell her that Jackie could go with them.

She said, "I don't want her to go. I need some adult time."

Jackie then planned to go with another aunt to a mall in Buffalo on Saturday, and on Sunday she was going to do some volunteer work. I still was not happy that she was relying on her aunts to keep her busy. On Friday morning Jackie texted me saying that her aunt could no longer take her to the mall on Saturday, but I didn't respond to it. I believed this was going to be too much for Jackie with the long weekend looming ahead of her. Her text said she didn't know how she was going to stay busy enough not to constantly be thinking about how homesick she was. The wheels fell off the cart.

Joe and I were hosting a brunch for thirty-five Duke students that Sunday, so I was out shopping when my phone rang. It was Joe. Jackie had called and asked him if she could fly home for the weekend.

At first I said, "Absolutely not!" I thought the cost of a ticket would be too expensive, and I simply didn't think she should come home. However, after some discussion and several phone calls back and forth, Joe shared that he thought perhaps we should let her come home. Most of the students at St. Bonaventure live within driving distance. His point was that if she lived close by, we would let her come home. This was a flight versus a drive in a car.

Late Friday night we met Jackie's flight. When she came down the stairs, she didn't even smile when she saw us. She looked thin and tired. Jackie had lost 10 pounds and clearly was not sleeping well.

Saturday was a good day. We went to the Duke/Navy football game. After returning home from the game, we again discussed the situation. Although Jackie got very emotional at times, she visibly relaxed as we talked about how she could make it through the semester. At that point, success was getting Jackie to complete the semester, and then we could talk about transferring to a school closer to home.

Sunday morning, we were up early getting ready for the brunch. A few hours later our guests began to arrive, and Jackie was sitting on the back porch. I asked how she was doing, and she said, "I can't go back."

When our company departed, I told Joe that we needed to talk. During the course of our discussion, we finally decided that it was best to not have Jackie return to Bonas. Quite honestly, we were concerned that if she returned, something more serious could develop, such as an eating disorder or a breakdown.

I went upstairs and sent an e-mail to the registrar to have Jackie withdrawn. My next e-mail was to Sister Margaret, the University President. I didn't want her to hear about this from anyone else. About ten minutes later the phone rang. It was Sister Margaret. She expressed great concern about Jackie and was sorry that being at Bonas didn't work out for her.

The following is the e-mail I sent to the family:

All -

I am very sad to inform you that we have made the decision to have Jackie withdraw from St. Bonaventure. Obviously, a very difficult and emotional decision.

Joe and Jackie will drive up to Olean on Thursday, move her out Friday and return to Cary on Saturday.

Thanks to all of you who tried to help Jackie deal with her homesickness.

Love,

Mo

The next few days were very emotional for Jackie. We would assure her that it would work out and that she needed to move forward. The next day, she began looking for a job, and then later in the week, Jackie and Joe drove up to Bonas. There was no way I could make that drive again! It was somewhat emotional, but she was happy when she moved out of her dorm room. Upon returning home Jackie had two job interviews and completed an application to begin school in January at a local college.

I had a Board meeting a couple of weeks later, and I didn't want to answer the 'How is Jackie doing?' question twenty-five times, so I sent the following e-mail. It sums up well all that we went through and the myriad emotions that accompanied the experience.

All -

Ahead of our upcoming board meeting, I wanted to let you know that my daughter Jackie has withdrawn from St. Bonaventure.

Needless to say, this was not anticipated and was a painful experience for all of us. In her first week on campus, it became readily apparent that she was extremely homesick. Counseling sessions, countless hours on the phone, texting and even a return visit to Olean by me were not enough to change the situation, so we decided as a family that Jackie should return home.

This was an eye-opening experience for me, not only as a parent, but as a board member.

What I discovered was that St. Bonaventure has a wonderful support system in place for students and families who go through this type of crisis and other crises as well. Jackie's counselor was always available and extremely helpful.

Joe and I also learned that this is a challenge that many families face when sending a child off to college.

Jackie is now interviewing for jobs and will be continuing her education at another college closer to home in January.

We all know how special St. Bonaventure is. What you should also know is that the unique Bonaventure spirit has helped our family through this challenging time. It is heartening to know that other families that we may never know will or have had similar support from the University family when they needed it most.

Regards,

Maureen

I loved being a member of the Board of Trustees at St. Bonaventure. The responses to the e-mail above truly demonstrate why my fellow trustees are wonderful individuals who know, understand, and live the Franciscan spirit.

Maureen,

Thank you for sharing this emotional experience. It goes without saying that with you as her mother, Jackie will also become a special individual. Good luck to her as she moves on.

Best,

Jim

Maureen,

I hope it all works out for Jackie. Parenting is another of life's mysteries at times isn't it. But in true Franciscan optimism, you have to think that all things happen for a reason and this will all sort out. Given the incredible history of the Keenans and Bonas, this must have been a tough thing for all, but you show your strength by sharing! Good luck and see you next week!

All the best,

Dick

Maureen: I'm sorry to hear that things did not work out for Jackie at St. Bonaventure. I realize this was a difficult and upsetting situation for all of you, as you note, but everything happens for a reason and I am certain, as I am sure you are, that in the end all will be right and good. Yours was a wonderful note and your acknowledgment of St. Bonaventure's support and spirit was special.

Best of everything to you, your husband and Jackie.

Tim

Maureen,

I was touched by your email about your daughter Jackie for a number of reasons. As a parent, I know how difficult it is to see your child in pain and unhappy. As a fellow passionate Bona grad, I know how much we want our children to have the opportunity to experience the remarkable journey we had at Bonas and how it can change your life. My oldest son Jack was set to start at Bonas this fall. On August 14, he informed us that he decided he never really wanted to go to Bonas and wouldn't be attending the University. The problem was that Bonas was the only school he applied to for admission. Jack is now interviewing for jobs and trying to figure out where he wants to go to school. I feel a sense of loss for him knowing that he will never have the Bonaventure experience, but I realize that may be more my adjustment than his. I know in the end that he and your daughter will be wonderful people no matter which path they choose. I just wanted you to know that I'm thinking of you and your family. I'll see you at the meeting.

Take care,

Gene

Maureen,

This very thing happened to the daughter of my good friend a couple of years ago. She is doing great in a local college right now. I guess we all move along the journey at our own pace—and that is good. Best of luck to Jackie.

I'm so glad to hear that the Bona support system worked so well!

See you in October.

Fr. Frank

Dear Maureen,

I'm another parent whose child left Bonas. It was a necessary and good move for him, and a clarifying time for him as he explored other possibilities. I will pray that this will be a clarifying time for Jackie, and am confident that when she looks back, this turn in the road will be seen as a blessed (not fun!) event, for her and for your family.

Your brother,

Bob

For several years, Jackie struggled with her post high school academic journey despite her attempts. It began to appear to us that academic work was not Jackie's thing, and she needed to find herself and the work she wanted to pursue along another path.

In spite of Jackie's school struggles, something very good did happen for her – she met her best friend and life partner. Jackie tells the story of walking down the hallway during her sophomore year at Cardinal Gibbons High School and seeing a junior boy wearing an Army sweatshirt. While she can be quite shy, she actually stopped and asked him where he got the sweatshirt. That was the first time Jackie spoke to Stephen Thorn.

Their relationship was typical of most high school romances. They began dating in 2006 during Jackie's sophomore year, which was Stephen's junior year. They continued dating through high school, Stephen's year at the United States Naval Academy Prep School, and into his second year at the United States Naval Academy (USNA). There was a break up that lasted for about eighteen months, but they reconnected during Stephen's junior year at USNA.

In February, 2011, Jackie and I were sitting at the kitchen table when she asked me what I would think if they got engaged. I began to cry.

Jackie, somewhat uncertain, said, "Are those happy tears?"

I said, "Yes, Jackie, these are happy tears."

A few months later, during his spring break, Stephen asked if he could come by the house and talk to Joe and me. We sat on the back porch on a beautiful spring day, and Stephen asked us if he could marry Jackie. It was a very special moment, and I was happy that I was included in the conversation. In June they were engaged.

Stephen graduated from the Naval Academy in May, 2012, and was commissioned into the Marine Corps. A month later he and

Jackie were married. They moved to Quantico, Virginia, where Stephen went through The Basic School and the Infantry Officer Course. When Stephen graduated from Quantico he was assigned to Marine Corps Base Hawaii.

Before they left for Hawaii, Jackie called to tell me she had been researching culinary schools. There was a school in Hawaii that had a baking program in which she was interested. I told Jackie that we still had some money in her college fund, and if she were accepted, we would pay the tuition; but she had to do all of the work to apply. Jackie applied and was accepted.

At the start of the program, I recall vividly a picture Jackie sent from her phone. She was holding the textbook that she would be using for the course. I remember thinking, *Here we go again*. About a month into the program, Jackie had her first test. She had studied hard but was quite nervous because of her past experiences in college. A few days later she received her results. Jackie's grade was a 97! This gave Jackie unbelievable confidence.

Jackie's program required a lot of hands-on experiences. Tests required the students to demonstrate their proficiency in various baking skills, including chocolate and sugar sculptures, candy making, cake decorating, French pastries, and other culinary delights. At the conclusion of each phase, the students would present their work to a panel of judges. The judges would confer, and then a gold medal was awarded to the student who had the best product.

Jackie received the gold medal in each category except one throughout the course of the program, and at the conclusion of the program, Jackie was awarded the Chef's Medal. This medal is presented to the student who demonstrated exceptional skills, and it is important to note that the medal is not awarded each year. After several starts and stops, Jackie earned her diploma!

A week after she graduated, the owner of a local boutique bakery called the baking school looking to hire a baker. Without hesitation they recommended Jackie. She interviewed and was accepted for the position. Jackie spent eighteen months honing her skills in Hawaii. Upon returning to the mainland, Jackie is now working in another bakery where she was recently named the manager of the back of the bakery, overseeing production and quality assurance. It turned out that Jackie is not only a baker, she is also a leader.

I gave a talk to a group of women sometime during this journey with Jackie. After the talk, a participant came up to me and said, "I know you have a daughter, why didn't you talk about her?"

I answered, "Right now I can't."

This period of time with Jackie was an emotional roller coaster. When we have children, we have hopes and dreams for them. For some of us those hopes and dreams never materialize.

Eventually, I was able to share Jackie's story. After another one of those talks, a woman came up and said, "I can't thank you enough for telling Jackie's story. All we ever hear is how perfect everyone's children are." She went on to say, "My children have struggled, too."

I learned how important it is to understand that everyone has his or her own journey. Additionally, everyone learns differently, and college is not for everyone. Jackie found her way.

I am very proud of Jackie!

JAY

In the military, commanders have special coins. Normally these coins have the unit symbol, motto, and other relevant information about the unit. Coins are given for excellence, and for some they are a big deal. I had a coin: one side had the DPE crest, and the other side had a sword and the words, 'Presented by the Master of the Sword.' I presented MOS coins to the Army officers when they departed after their tour and to the civilians faculty members after they had completed three years in the department. Additionally, I would give the coins to cadets when they did something exceptional such as having the highest physical fitness test scores for their class.

Shortly after I had my retirement ceremony, my son Jay, who was a plebe at West Point at the time, said to me, "Mom, you never gave me your coin."

I said, "Jay you have not achieved excellence yet. When you do, I will give you my coin."

Harsh? I don't think so. It is all about standards. I had only given my coin to cadets who had achieved excellence. Jay was a cadet, and I thought it was important to hold him to the same standard. Jay's plebe year was rough academically, and as a result he had to spend a great deal of time studying and did not perform as well physically. He had passed his physical education courses, but never maxed (achieved the maximum score) the Army Physical Fitness Test (APFT).

We saw Jay prior to our departure from West Point in early June 2004. I said, "Jay, are you going to try to earn the RECONDO badge during Cadet Field Training (CFT)?"

He responded, "Mom, it's tough, I'm not sure I'll be able to do it."

I was irritated with him. I wanted him to tell me that he would work hard and at least try.

CFT is the six-week military summer training program following the plebe year. The cadets are off post at Camp Buckner. "Cadet Field Training (CFT) introduces cadets to the close ground fight and the associated challenges of leading soldiers in a tactical environment."[16]

---

[16] DMI website accessed December 10, 2004; 6:00 a.m.

Within the first few days, the cadets take the APFT. Jay called home. He had maxed it! This was the first step toward earning the RECONDO badge. The cadet leadership that Jay had during the first half of CFT were excellent; they motivated Jay and the members of his company. With the success of each event, Jay would work harder so that he could stay in the hunt for the RECONDO badge.

The RECONDO badge is earned by thirty-two to thirty-five percent of the cadets for achieving a high standard on the Army Physical Fitness Test, which included: day and night land navigation; weapons tasks; confidence obstacle course; fire support; record obstacle course; endurance run; poncho raft swim; water obstacle course; and RECONDO stakes.

Early one August morning, the phone rang. It was Jay. "Hi Mom. I called to tell you that I'm looking at a shiny RECONDO badge."

Not one to assume anything, "Whose chest is the shield pinned on?" I asked.

The response, "Mine!"

I was thrilled for Jay! He had tasted success after a very difficult plebe year.

Jay came home for a visit in early October, and he looked great – healthy, strong, and of course, handsome. I gave him a big hug, and when we had a quiet moment together, I gave him my coin. It's all about standards! I'm confident that the coin is more meaningful to Jay because he had to earn it; I didn't just give it to him. No doubt, this was a good lesson about the importance of maintaining standards for a future leader.

Mom with eight children, 1958. Left to right, front row, Maureen, Bob, Birdie (baby), Connie, Dee Dee, back row, Timer, Kathy, Judie.

First picture of Mom and Dad with all nine children, 1960. Left to right front row, Connie, Birdie, Bob, Judie, Dee Dee, Maureen, back row, Kathy, Mom, Kevin (infant), Dad, Timer.

Getting ready to make a splash! Poolside at the Bartlett Country Club.
Left to right, Kevin, Birdie, Connie, Dee Dee, Maureen, Bob, Judie, Kathy,
Timer.

After the last surgery on my
right arm, January 1961.

Six girls, 1962. Kathy is in the center, left to right, Connie, Dee Dee, Judie, Maureen, and sweet little Birdie.

The pink Easter dresses with the daisies! Left to right front row, Judie, Connie, Birdie, Bob, Kevin & Timer. Back row, Dee Dee, Mom, Maureen and Kathy. March 26, 1967.

Dee Dee, Birdie, Connie and Maureen with Coach Matt Conte, our Bartlett Country Club swim coach. We had just won the champion-ship at Callahan Pool in Bradford, Pennsylvania.

Similar to the red ribbon Judie brought home that inspired me to join the Bartlett Country Club swim team.

This picture appeared in the *Olean Times Herald*, October 1973. Maureen is first from the left, and Maureen's sister Dee Dee is fourth from the left.

Getting ready to board a UH-1H at St. Bonaventure University - October 1973.

Summer 1975 at Fort McClellan, Alabama. I am the back center.

Graduation day, St. Bonaventure University, May 1976.

Second lieutenant bars being pinned by LTC Dunn, the Professor of Military Science at St. Bonaventure on the left, and my dad on the right.

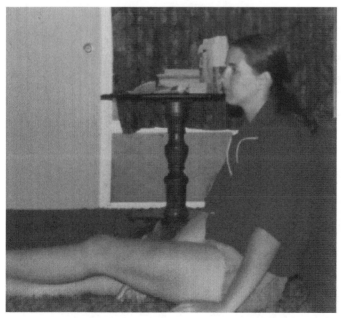

In a hotel somewhere in Tennessee the night before I reported for active duty at Fort McClellan, Alabama.

My platoon at Fort McClellan AL. That's me in the top row, fourth from the right, 1976.

Swearing in Connie and Dee Dee as second lieutenants in the U.S. Army with Mom and Dad proudly looking on, May 1977.

With Mom standing next to a TH-55 at Fort Rucker, Alabama, Spring 1980.

At the controls of a UH-1 in Germany, 1981.

During a field exercise in Germany, 1982.

Briefing the VII Corps Support Commander during a field exercise in Germany, 1982. I was the 394th Transportation Battalion's S1/personnel officer.

The sabre arch after our wedding ceremony, July 17, 1982.

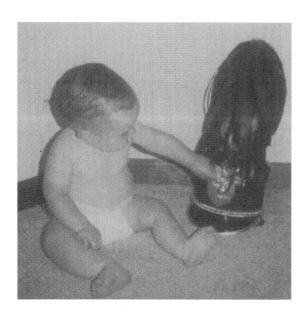

Jay with Joe's tar bucket, the cadet headgear worn during parades at West Point.

My promotion ceremony to Major. COL Anderson, the Master of the Sword, presided with my dad standing by ready to pin on my new rank. Notice Jay in the background playing with the flag.

Department of Physical Education Faculty 1986. This was taken when I was an instructor in DPE. I'm in the second row from the top, fifth from the left.

Team LeBoeuf at Fort Carson,
Colorado, 1990.

LeBoeuf family at the U.S. Army War College, 1996.

With Jay, the Plebe (freshman), after my advancement to Brigadier General, April 2004.

Jay after graduating from Airborne school, July 2005.

Jay's USMA graduation, May 26, 2007. This was a very special day in our family to see Jay continue in the "family business" as he entered the Army profession.

Jay returns from Iraq on his twenty-sixth birthday at Fort Riley, Kansas, July, 2010.

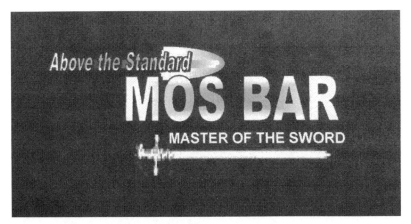

Master of the Sword bar. A simple, yet powerful way to recognize excellence within the Department of Physical Education.

The obverse side of my Master of the Sword coin.

The reverse side of my Master of the Sword coin. These were given out sparingly.

My New York license plate while I was the Master of the Sword. There was no doubt on the grounds of West Point who drove this car.

Meeting President George W. Bush prior to West Point graduation, June 1, 2002. It's always a thrill to meet the Commander-in-Chief.

Speaking at a ceremony at Trophy Point, a scenic overlook located on the grounds of West Point.

A seven-mile run referred to as the "runback" from Camp Buckner to West Point with the rising Yearlings (sophomores). I am at the front of the formation.

Another year, another runback. These were always great fun and built esprit-de-corps. The current Master of the Sword, COL Nick Gist, is over my right shoulder.

The DPE faculty 2002 Howitzer Yearbook photo. A wonderful group of educators committed to educating, developing and inspiring the future leaders of our Army.

With some of the DPE officers. It was a privilege to serve with such wonderful leaders and athletes.

Unveiling DPE's Strategic Vision. Dr. Ralph Vernacchia looks on. He was instrumental in the development of the vision and the strategic plan.

Presenting the DPE flag to BG Leo Brooks, the Commandant of Cadets.

My stars being pinned on by Joe, Jay and Jackie – April 2004.

My brother Timer with me at my retirement ceremony. I retired as a General, he retired as a Colonel, he does NOT call me ma'am!

DPE faculty circa 1937-38. This picture was given to me by Mrs. Joanne Holbrook Patton, General George Patton's daughter-in-law. Mrs. Patton's father, William A. Holbrook, Jr., was the Master of the Sword 1934-1938. He is seated in the first row, second from the left.

Jackie with her textbook as she was getting ready to begin her baking and pastry arts program in Honolulu, Hawaii.

Jackie's graduation from baking school. This was a wonderful day when Jackie successfully completed her program. She had a lot of success as you can see by all of the medals she received.

Leading a cheer for Miss Martha Altmire at her retirement from Olean High School. She was the cheerleading advisor my senior year. Once a cheerleader, always a cheerleader.

Speaking at my high school alma mater, Olean High School, in Olean, New York.

After a Revitalizing America event hosted by UBS with former U.S. Presidents Bill Clinton and George W. Bush.

Since leaving the Army I do a lot of speaking about the importance of a leadership philosophy and moments that matter. I simply love this work!

CHAPTER SIX

DEPARTMENT OF PHYSICAL EDUCATION – MY SECOND TOUR

BECOMING DIRECTOR OF INSTRUCTION

When I returned to West Point and DPE in 1994, I had the title Director of Instruction (DOI). My job was to oversee the physical education curriculum for the 4,400 members of the Corps of Cadets. Physical education is not taken lightly at USMA; in fact, it has a long and storied tradition.

The Academy was founded in 1802, and it has been reported that West Point was the first institution in higher education in the United States to hire a full-time physical educator.[17] In 1814, Pierre Thomas, a sword master, was hired to teach fencing to the cadets. Since that time, the position of the Director and Head of the Department of Physical Education carries with it the unique title 'Master of the Sword.' In the early years, the cadets also took horseback riding, and

---

[17] Degen, R. (1968). The Evolution of Physical Education at the United States Military Academy, 20, United States Military Academy, West Point, New York.

eventually dance was added to the curriculum. In a document dated May 8, 1928, there was an attempt to abolish the Master of the Sword title and change it to Director of Physical Training. Actually, the full title was 'Master of the Sword and Senior Instructor in Military Gymnastics and Physical Culture.'[18] Now, that's a title!

The Physical Program, as it is called, is a four-year developmental, sequential, integrated program. Each year during their four years, cadets take physical education courses, participate in athletics, and take various fitness tests. During my time there, survival swimming, military movement, and combatives were the physical education courses for the plebes. Also, the men took boxing, and the women took self-defense.

Having served as an instructor previously in DPE, I was excited to return to USMA as the person who would oversee the physical education curriculum, the very best physical education program in higher education in the country! I have said this in front of my counterparts and friends at both the Air Force and Naval Academies, and they never disagreed.

The department had undergone some changes during the six years I was gone. However, most of the change was occurring as I was returning to join the permanent faculty. A department reorganization, a reduction in force, and the moving of five civilian faculty members and their families out of government quarters were in the works. A Ph.D. requirement for the civilian faculty was being added to the USMA Faculty Manual as well as the adoption of the five domains (scholarship, teaching, service, cadet development, and faculty development) as the criteria to evaluate faculty performance and serve as the basis for promotion. Total Quality Army (TQA), which is similar to Total Quality Management, was being adopted, and the

---

[18] Official correspondence dated May 8, 1928. Subject: Abolishing the title "Master of the Sword".

department structure went from hierarchical to a nearly flat line. Any one of these changes addressed independently was significant, but all occurring simultaneously was, in a word, overwhelming.

The day I returned to DPE there was a meeting. I sat down next to one of the senior civilian faculty members and said, "Hello, how are you doing?" He said, "Not good. Before this (referring to the housing situation) is all over, I will probably be in jail!" In the moment I wasn't quite sure what he was referring to; however, I thought, *Welcome back to DPE.*

The reorganization and the reduction in force (or RIF) caused significant turmoil in the department. For several years the Office of the Directorate of Intercollegiate Athletics (ODIA)[19] had been operating in the red. The recommended and adopted solution to the problem was to move some of the coaches to DPE so that they could both coach and teach. As a part of the reorganization, there were full-time DPE faculty who had to take on coaching duties and coaches who had to take on teaching duties. The change resulted in the creation of seventeen Instructor/Coaches (I/C) in DPE, and I was their immediate supervisor.

The Academy had been directed by Congress to begin hiring more civilian faculty. USMA was required to have twenty to twenty-five percent of its faculty comprised of civilians. DPE had always had a large number of civilian faculty members, but this was a significant change for almost all of the academic departments. As a result, there was a change in the way the faculty would be evaluated, paid, and titled. The law changed from Title 5 to Title 10, and along with the

---

[19] The Office of the Directorate of Intercollegiate Athletics and the Department of Physical Education are separate organizations. While both directors are responsible for a portion of the Physical Education Program, they have different bosses. The Director of ODIA reports directly to the USMA Superintendent (president of the school), and the Head of DPE reports directly to the Commandant of Cadets (similar to a Dean of Students.)

change in the law was the addition of academic titles. For example, instead of being a GS (Government Servant) 12, based on the faculty member's academic credentials, s/he was reclassified as an Instructor, Assistant Professor, Associate Professor, or Professor.

Since there were not a lot of civilian faculty members at USMA, when they were promoted to the rank of GS12, they were authorized to live on the grounds of West Point in government housing. Once it became apparent that USMA was going to have to hire many more civilians, the Superintendent gave the civilians living in government housing ninety days to vacate their homes, vice grandfathering them and allowing them to stay in their quarters. They had to move off the grounds of West Point. There were five members of the DPE faculty who were impacted by this decision, and frankly they were quite angry, feeling that their contract with the Academy has been seriously violated. This became a significant issue for me in my role because it was as if I were to blame for this change.

The domains of scholarship, teaching and service were not new to those actively involved in higher education. However, the Ph.D. requirement and the addition of research and scholarship were very new to the DPE faculty and would create a significant work requirement in an already heavy workload. The rotating military and civilian faculty all had master's degrees, only a few of the civilians had doctorates. The head of the department, the deputy, and I all had doctorates.

Additionally, as a result of all of the negativity in the department, the Director decided to add a sixth domain, organizational citizenship, as a means to hold members of the faculty to a higher standard of behavior. The definition of organizational citizenship as it was used in DPE was as follows:

The operating principles of the United States Military Academy and the Department of Physical Education are grounded in a code of ethics, values and behavior. This code is a guide for the faculty when performing their duties and interacting with faculty, staff and cadets in a professional capacity. Organizational Citizenship is a personal expression of an individual's commitment to departmental, institutional goals, and Department of Army values and ethics in the work environment.[20]

With the adoption of TQA, the focus was on the team with no one officially designated to be in charge of a given team. All decisions were made through a team consensus.

I remember vividly a conversation I had with the officer who, prior to my arrival, was the previous DOI, and who was now serving as the deputy of the department. He came into my office and informed me that the fall teaching schedule needed to be published; essentially, who was going to be teaching what courses and when they would be teaching. Prior to TQA, this would have been a fairly easy task. I would have called the person responsible for all of the classes for the sophomores through seniors or the Upper Class Director and the Fourth Class Director, the person responsible for the freshman courses. I would have told them what I want, they would have gotten with the course directors, and within a couple of days I would have had the information. However, now that we had TQA, scheduling of the faculty was quite different.

I asked him if there was a list with the names of the instructors, what they were qualified to teach, and when they were available. It was a job he should have done. To my absolute amazement and chagrin, the answer was no. He told me to get with the course directors. However, with TQA in place as an operational process, no one person was in charge, nor titled as the course director. I went from having to deal with two individuals to now having to deal with

---

[20] Memorandum for Department of Physical Education Civilian Faculty; Subject: Merit Evaluation Plan for Academic Year 1996-97; 11 February 1997.

every faculty member in the department, or at best, teams of faculty members.

I sent out an e-mail message that essentially stated that while I knew no one person was in charge, I needed a point of contact for each course. Otherwise, I would assign instructors where and when I wanted them to teach. As you can imagine, a boxing instructor did not want to be assigned to teach swimming. I eventually received the information I needed, but it was not done in a smooth and timely manner. I did not feel as though I was off to a good start, and I had only recently returned.

IT WAS THE WORST OF TIMES

There was an incredible amount of anger within the department. The civilian faculty members who had taught in the department and had lived in government quarters, many for years, were asked to change their jobs, potentially required to earn a Ph.D., and, in some cases, move out of their homes. There were several lawsuits filed against the Academy by some of the DPE civilian faculty.[21] My first meeting with the Commandant of Cadets was to discuss an issue surrounding one of the lawsuits.

The two years that I served as the Director of Instruction were, by far, the worst two years of my Army career! The issues I have briefly described were horrific, and because I was the first-line supervisor for all of the Instructor/Coaches, as well as some of the military faculty, I felt attacked from all sides daily – it was relentless. People were so angry. While I had not been at the Academy when these decisions were made, for some it didn't matter. I was *management*, a word I dislike because I strongly believe we lead people and manage resources. Unfortunately, for those whom I supervised, I was seen as

---

[21] The civilian faculty won none of the lawsuits.

one of the creators and owners of the problem. Their anger was being directed at me.

I set up a series of initial counseling sessions at the start of the academic year. The sessions gave me an opportunity to review each individual's goals and objectives for the year, and it also gave me a chance to get to know my people better. I had blocked thirty to forty-five minutes on my calendar for each session. After the first few, I realized I needed to block at least two hours. People were angry and upset. They needed an opportunity to talk, to vent their anger, but more importantly, they needed someone to actually listen and empathize with their situation and point of view.

The Instructor/Coaches had busy days; they were expected to teach as well as coach, both at a very high standard of performance. The civilian faculty had to use time cards. Each week they would report their hours to an administrative assistant, and it was normally a forty-hour workweek. I have to admit, I had trouble with individuals whom I considered professionals being required to keep time cards. Frankly, professionals train and educate to standard, and not to time. And, high standards take a lot of time.

Because we had a budget with limited resources for pay, if a faculty member had overtime hours, they were allocated compensatory time or time off. Some of the I/Cs were diligent about reporting the time worked. Time was logged if a coach were sitting on a bus headed to an away competition. One I/C logged so much time that he did not work in DPE for the entire summer; however, he did perform all of his coaching duties. You can easily imagine the kind of problems and equity challenges this system created.

One day, one of the coaches asked if he could talk to me about what it takes to recruit one athlete. I agreed to the conversation. I was interested. He came into my office with a rather thick file and explained the process. We spent a few hours together. He talked, I listened, I asked questions, and he answered. At the conclusion of the meeting, I certainly had a much better understanding of that single aspect of coaching and the fundamental bind we had created with our system of accountability for time. As he left, he thanked me for my time. I suspect that after this meeting, he told other coaches that we had met. While I certainly did not understand all aspects of coaching, I had a better understanding of what it takes to recruit an athlete at the Military Academy. However, the bottom line here is that I listened.

Now, here is a story that I have rarely shared. As this was going on, I'm not sure I even told my husband.

At times in DPE I feared for my physical safety! There was one individual who was extremely angry over all that had gone on in the department. His anger was palpable. As he walked through the halls of the department, if he saw me, he would try not to speak. I have trouble with someone not speaking when spoken to. It's about dignity and respect. He would send e-mails, several each day, and all tagged so that he knew when I opened them. I would respond and then another e-mail would come. It became a relentless cycle of communication.

Eventually, I slowed down my responses to him. I would respond to his e-mails a few times a week, not several times each day. No doubt this probably irritated him. At faculty meetings he actually sat sideways in his chair so as not to look at the department head. The lack of respect he demonstrated, under conditions that were difficult for everyone, was over the top, suggesting a deep lack of trust, and something that I never experienced in my military career. Being angry was one thing, but the unwillingness to work to reduce this anger and find a positive way forward was unacceptable.

In DPE, a survival swimming class is taught, and rubber M-16s are utilized. It was not unusual for someone to walk through the hallways with one of these replica weapons. I honestly thought that if this individual walked into the department with a real weapon, no one would have noticed until it was too late. Yes, he seemed that angry to me.

When I left the department each night, it was through a tunnel in the back of the building. The tunnel was dark, not well-lit, and during the winter months, it was very dark. I always walked down the middle of the tunnel so that if anyone came at me, I would at least see an attack coming. Yes! I was afraid! There will be some who will read this, especially those who were in the department at the time, and think this was silly. However, this was how I felt; it was my reality!

Fortunately, in the summer of 1996, Joe and I packed up the children and headed to Carlisle, Pennsylvania, where Joe and I would attend the Army War College, whose motto is: 'Not to promote war, but to preserve peace.' A little peace sounded good; it was exactly the break I needed from all that was going on in DPE.

Prior to my departure, I made sure that the individual who would serve as the Acting DOI had a continuity notebook that would guide him through all of the actions for the academic year. In fact, the faculty assignments for the fall semester were already made.

I knew there would be even bigger changes when I returned from the War College. The current head of the department would have to retire by the end of the 1996-97 academic year.[22] He had served faithfully in the position for the previous twenty-three years. The current deputy had arrived in 1995 and, in my opinion, was the heir apparent to be the next head of DPE. He had a Ph.D. and had graduated from the Army War College; he was fully qualified to become the next Master of the Sword.

---

[22] Professors in USMA can serve until the first of the month following their 64th birthday.

U.S. Army War College and the Notification

Shortly after my arrival at the War College, the position for the Director and Head of the Department of Physical Education was advertised in the *Army Times*. After many long and thoughtful discussions with my husband, I decided that I would go ahead and apply. I believed it would be good for my professional development. It would be good for me to put a resume together and prepare for and go through the interview process. In the military, one rarely interviews for a position; rather, one is assigned.

The deputy called one afternoon in early September and told me that he was not going to apply for the position; he was going to retire. *The deputy was not going to apply*? I was surprised. He did offer to write a letter of recommendation for my packet, which I accepted.

I have often been asked, "How long had you thought about becoming the Master of the Sword? When did it become a goal?"

I have to admit becoming the Master of the Sword was not a long-standing career goal, in large part because I never thought that I would be in a position to be considered for the job, largely because of timing and because I'm not a USMA grad. And, oh yes, I'll say it, I'm a woman. The day the deputy called and said he was not applying was the very first time I ever thought I could be selected.

I was familiar with the others who would be applying and would be seriously considered for the position. I knew that none had a doctorate, and none had graduated from the Army War College. I would be the only person applying who had both the civilian and military academic credentials along with recent experience in the department. I completed my packet, mailed it, and was notified that I would be interviewed in early December 1996.

The Call

As mentioned in this book's introduction, I was not expecting the phone call that I received in February 1997, thinking I had time to prepare to receive the call that I thought would be weeks or possibly months away. When I heard the Commandant's voice that day telling me that I'd been selected as the next Master of the Sword, I was truly speechless and so incredibly thrilled.

There were some great officers who had also been considered, so the appointment was truly an honor, and the selection was not lost on me. This was truly historic for the Military Academy. I was the first woman to be selected to be the Director and Head of the Department of Physical Education. However, equally as noteworthy, I became the first woman to chair any department in the history of the United States Military Academy.[23] At the time, West Point was 195 years old!

While I was thrilled at my selection, many of the 'Old Grads' were not. I often joke that there was a tremor in the Northeast the day the Commandant called me with the news; it was the Old Grads rolling in their graves at West Point. Old Grad is an affectionate term used for any graduate of West Point. One becomes an Old Grad the moment they are handed their diploma. The response to my selection did turn rather interesting. There was a group of Old Grads who actively tried to block my nomination and appointment as the Master of the Sword.

I was home in Olean, on leave prior to assuming my duties at West Point, when I received a call from a general officer who is also a close Army friend. He told me that there was an e-mail campaign started by a few West Point graduates who were retired generals and were trying to interfere with the process. He asked if I wanted to see the e-mail. I said, "Sir, I don't want to see anything negative, I only

---

[23] USMA celebrated its bicentennial in 2002.

want to be surrounded by the positive when I take over DPE." I already knew that there were a lot of tough internal issues facing me when I returned to DPE; I did not want any external issues distracting me from my primary focus, leading the Department of Physical Education.

While I did not want or need to see the e-mail, eventually it was shared with me by the Public Affairs Officer at the time. The West Point Association of Graduates is made up of West Point Societies, which are groups of West Point graduates located around the world. One joins their local West Point Society. The following communication was sent to the West Point Society Presidents on June 9, 1997. Below is a portion of the e-mail:

> *"For all*
>
> *Two graduates have initiated an effort to request the Senate Armed Services committee to direct the USMA to reopen the bidding for the permanent position of Director of Physical Education (Master of the Sword.) What follows is a suggested letter prepared by* ███████████████████████████████████ *. The course of action is similar to the letter-writing campaign of some few years ago which saved Doubleday Field. The current composition of the SASC is appended for your use, but the letter may be sent with appropriate modification to any Senator. Further, the text may be personalized as the writer sees fit.*
>
> *Begin proposed text*
>
> *Dear Senator (   )*
>
> *I am writing to you in your role as a member of the Armed Services Committee regarding the situation which many people feel is improper and may violate Federal hiring regulations. It concerns the recent selection by the United States Military*

Academy of a replacement for the retiring permanent Professor of Physical Education at West Point. The position is subject to confirmation by the Senate.

I believe that the selection process was conducted in an improper manner and that the selectee may not be the best qualified for the position.

The selection process was not advertised properly or widely. It is my understanding that it appeared briefly in the Army Times and not advertised in appropriate higher education journals. There was (sic) a small number of applicants, but many highly qualified individuals were unaware of the position vacancy.

The selected person is the spouse of a permanent associate professor of another academic department at the Academy who was in a position to influence the selection process, hence there is a perception of possible conflict of interest.

The Department of Physical Education is one of the most important departments at the Military Academy. It influences every cadet every week of the four years as no other department does. The P.E. Department is responsible for training and preparing cadets to physically lead United States soldiers in combat. This is a highly visible department furthering the 'combat leader' mission of the Academy.

In past years, it was a requirement that this department be led by an officer who had commanded at the Battalion level and who was deemed qualified to lead in combat. This nominee does not meet this criteria.

For the above reasons, I respectfully request that Academy authorities be directed to reopen the selection process.

End proposed text

A list of the serving Republicans and Democrats of the Senate Armed Services Committee followed the proposed text.

My only comment about this proposed e-mail was that suggesting that my husband would have been able to influence the selection process was laughable.

Becoming The Master of the Sword

If my previous two years in the Department of Physical Education were the worst two years in my Army career, what was I thinking? Why would I ever want to go in as the Director and Head of the Department of Physical Education? It was easy. I knew the problems in the department, I had dealt with them daily, and maybe, just maybe, I could go in and make a difference.

I gave a lot of thought to the way in which I would lead DPE. I had a few months before I became the head of the department, and I took advantage of the time to reflect on the current situation and look forward. Fortunately, while I was at the War College, I took an elective course, Philosophy of Leadership, in which we had the opportunity to read, discuss, and reflect on the topic. During the course, I wrote a paper with the target audience of mid-level to senior-level leaders. However, leaders at all levels can benefit from this article, titled, *Developing a Leadership Philosophy.*[24]

As a part of the preparation for writing the paper, I reviewed the papers of others who had taken the Philosophy of Leadership course during previous years. As I reviewed the papers, several common themes emerged regarding what should be included in a leadership philosophy. They were vision, values, caring, leader development, managing change, diversity, and a sense of humor.

---

[24] http://www.au.af.mil/au/awc/awcgate/milreview/leboeuf.htm.

160

I did a deep dive into my values and what was important to me. I reflected on the stories of my life and the experiences that have shaped me into the person I am today.

Prior to arriving back in DPE, I sat down and wrote my leadership philosophy using some of the aforementioned themes and adding others to shape my leadership point of view and my philosophy. The leadership philosophy I developed for my role as the Master of the Sword served me well for seven years. It was the first topic of conversation I had with the staff and faculty of DPE. Additionally, I reviewed it each time I sat down with a new member of the department and made sure that it still fit. I made one addition over the years, and that was the addition of wellness.

The leadership philosophy I used is in Appendix A. Each of the tenets of my leadership philosophy is used as the framework for the next section of this book. Additionally, I used stories from my personal experiences that illustrate how I walked the talk, and how I lived my leadership philosophy.

I do not believe in making change for change's sake. However, I was certain that I needed to make some visible changes to illustrate there was a new Master of the Sword. Remember, I was replacing someone who had been in the position for twenty-three years.

As mentioned earlier, DPE has a large number of civilian faculty members; almost fifty percent are civilians. The senior leadership structure in the department at the time was all military – the Director, the Deputy, and the Director of Instruction. I asked the department head if he would allow me to make some changes to the organization prior to my arrival. He is a real gentleman, and he agreed. I named a well-respected senior civilian professor as the new Director of Instruction. Because a senior army officer had always filled this position, I felt that this would send a strong message to the civilian faculty that they were valued, and they would be listened to and be represented as part of my leadership team.

Small Changes

Upon arrival, I chose to start by making some initial changes with my office décor. It had dark paneling from floor to ceiling. I asked the maintenance personnel to cut off the top half of the paneling and paint the wall a light color. It gave the office a brighter, cleaner feel. I also had some of the signage changed in the department.

There was a very small wooden sign with the words, *The Department of Physical Education,* hung near the entrance on a very large space. We went to the USMA signage office and asked for a large sign that would read, *Welcome to the Department of Physical Education.*

Of course, nothing is free, or so I thought until I asked how much the sign was going to cost. The gentleman said, "No one has asked for any signage in DPE in a long time, so for you, no charge." The new, large sign replaced the smaller sign, and it was a big improvement.

Another change was to the uniforms we wore. In DPE, the uniform consisted of black polyester pants with a small white stripe down the side and a grey three-button polyester shirt with the DPE crest on the right side. They were hideous and had been worn in the department for decades. I established a uniform committee to come to me with recommendations on a new and improved uniform.

The first change to the uniform was a new rain jacket with a state-of-the-art reflective fabric and our names and the DPE crest embroidered on the chest. It was a sharp, very professional appearing jacket. The committee took their time, since there were a lot of uniform items that had to be selected. For example, the uniform we wore outside of the department or around West Point went from black polyester to khaki pants and a materially improved shirt. I felt that we, as a faculty, looked more professional, and the uniforms were much more functional. These small changes had, in my mind, large effects on how we viewed ourselves as a faculty and as an organization.

There was some media attention when I first arrived as the Master of the Sword. After all, I was the first woman to chair a department at the Military Academy since it was founded in 1802, one hundred ninety-five years earlier. During an interview with a reporter for the *Pointer View*, the on-post newspaper, the reporter said she had talked to some cadets about my appointment, and a woman cadet said, "They will run her off in a year." I didn't respond to the comment, but I was sad and disappointed that a woman cadet thought that would happen.

In the summer months, DPE facilitates various physical training events with the rising yearlings (sophomores) during Cadet Field Training. One morning, they were going to participate in a biathlon, a swim followed by a run, and I went out to not only observe but to join in. There was a film crew waiting to film me as I exited the water, and they continued to film while I put on my running shoes in preparation for continuing the biathlon. The cameraman jumped into the back of a pickup truck, placed the camera on his shoulder, and filmed as I ran behind the truck. I don't like this kind of attention and told my husband I felt like a monkey in a circus act. He reminded me that this was part of the deal, and eventually the newness of me as the Master of the Sword would fade. He was correct. Over time, it wasn't as big a deal.

Invisible No Longer

I did not realize that when I became the Master of the Sword I would no longer be invisible. During my previous assignment in DPE as a lieutenant colonel, I wasn't very well known; there are a lot of lieutenant colonels at West Point. That all changed when I became the MOS.

One morning I was leaving one of our facilities, and as I was getting into my car, a man came running up to me and said, "Ma'am, I'm a big military history buff, and since you are now a part of the Military Academy's history, I want to shake your hand." I asked him his name, and we shook hands. The attention didn't end there.

Another time, I was traveling in uniform, had boarded a plane and taken my seat, when a gentleman said to me, "Can I sit next to the Master of the Sword?"

In DC eating breakfast one morning, the gentleman at the next table said, "Aren't you the Master of the Sword?"

Even after I retired and was on vacation in St. Thomas with my daughter Jackie, a couple walked past us and the wife said, "Aren't you the Master of the Sword?"

Jackie looked at me with eyebrows raised and said, "Wow!"

It was a little bit unnerving, but it was always a welcome reminder of my unique opportunity to serve.

On Saturday mornings, I would make a quick trip to Dunkin Donuts® to purchase bagels and, yes, donuts. People stationed at West Point would come walking in with smiles on their faces and then they would see me, the Master of the Sword, standing in line. Their expressions would change almost every time, and they almost always seemed compelled to explain to me why they were getting donuts.

I often heard, "Hi Ma'am, we have company, so I had to come and get some donuts." It was always quite amusing around the associations and expectations my role created.

At West Point, there are all the conveniences of a regular community, as in all military installations, including a post office, a post exchange (which is similar to a department store), and the commissary, which is the grocery store. I began to notice that other commissary shoppers would look in my cart to see what groceries I was purchasing. What does the Master of the Sword eat? Sometimes I would throw in a box of chocolate covered Ding-Dongs for fun and to cause a bit of a buzz.

Whenever I had dinner with my fellow department heads, when the dessert was served, someone would always say, "Oh I can't eat dessert in front of the Master of the Sword."

I would say, "Great! Then give it to me!"

A confession, I love sweets and desserts. Almost every evening while growing up we had a family dinner, and at the conclusion of the dinner Dad would say to Mom, "Ann, what lovely dessert have you prepared for us this evening?"

Sometimes it was as simple as Oreos, fruit cocktail in Jell-O, or warm brownie pudding, which is delicious. We had dessert almost every night. Did I mention that I love sweets? Fortunately for me I have worked out most of my life, have a good metabolism, and have been successful at controlling my consumption of sweets.

BIGGER CHANGES

Changing the uniforms was one thing, but making a change to USMA's storied boxing program was something totally different. Big changes that move in the face of embedded tradition are much more challenging.

Boxing is a course that has come under a great deal of scrutiny over the years, particularly in the current context of closed head injuries that have long-term, negative consequences. Many people do not believe men should box, let alone women. One of my male infantry officers came to me and asked if women could box. He was the coach of the club boxing team, and there were some women who had expressed an interest in participating in the sport. This was one

165

of those decisions that I knew I had to ask approval for. Brigadier General John Abizaid[25] was the Commandant of Cadets and my boss at the time. When I asked him, I honestly expected him to say no. He said, "Maureen, if you can determine a safe way to make this happen, then come back to me, and we will discuss it."

We started to talk about it in the department, and someone asked a very simple question. "What is required for a man to become a member of the club boxing team?"

The answer, "They have to take boxing."

I went to General Abizaid and recommended that the women take boxing. If a woman wanted to be a member of the club boxing team, she had to find a woman in her weight class and take the 19-lesson course. The boxing instructor would determine if the woman had the skills to join the boxing team upon completing the course. I shared this with General Abizaid who agreed and approved the decision to allow women to box at USMA. We implemented the change and did not make a big deal about it — no media, nothing. We simply let the women start boxing. I always believed that the young women who took boxing in order to allow a friend the opportunity to be on the club team truly demonstrated selfless service.

The first woman to box outside the gates of USMA was Jen Blatty, the captain of the women's Army Tennis Team. One Saturday morning, she participated in and won her tennis match. Later that day, she traveled to Lock Haven State College in Pennsylvania where she had a boxing match. Jen won that, too!

The next logical step for women in boxing at USMA was the chance to participate in the Brigade Open. The Brigade Open in boxing is a significant annual event on the West Point activities calendar.

---

[25] General John Abizaid was the 66th Commandant of Cadets at the United States Military Academy.

This event is open to all cadets in the corps, and has elimination bouts (based on weight class) in the weeks leading up to the big event. Additionally, as a risk management measure, cadets must have a certain level of skill in boxing, or the officer-in-charge will not allow a cadet to box. When a cadet wins the Brigade Open, he or she has bragging rights as the champion for a year, and frankly throughout their lives.

On December 10th, 2000, Cadets Erin Searfoss and Patricia Kast boxed in the 45th United States Military Academy Brigade Open. Because of the headgear and their relatively high skill level, it was not readily apparent to most of the audience that these were two women who were boxing. Erin won the bout, and now has the honor of being the first woman Brigade Boxing champion.

For the Class of 2020, boxing became mandatory for all cadets, men and women. Fundamentally, what took place in 2000 was, and continued to make, a significant change in the male-dominated tradition of the Military Academy.

During the time I was the MOS, cadets took two physical education courses as yearlings (sophomores) that focused on enhancing physical readiness, self-confidence, and overall wellness. Close Quarters Combat was the fourth combatives course that the cadets took. In this nineteen-lesson, gender-integrated course, the cadets were exposed to "...a comprehensive set of unarmed combat skills, and the strategies and tactics needed to neutralize a physical attack. Responses to a striking, kicking, joint locking, choking, throwing, and ground grappling attack are taught with an emphasis on submission holds applied on the ground as finishing techniques."[26]

The wellness course exposed the cadets to myriad topics in the areas of social, emotional, spiritual, physical, environmental, and mental. The cadets not only learned the importance of these issues

---

[26] Department of Physical Education (2003). Physical Program (Whitebook). West Point, NY.

on a personal level for themselves, but as future leaders, they learned the importance of these issues as they applied to their teams.

As cows[27] (juniors), the cadets took a personal fitness course and participated in a lifetime sport as an elective. Personal fitness built on some of what was taught in wellness; however, the primary focus of the course was physical fitness. Through a study of basic physiology, the cadets learned about the five components of fitness: muscular strength, muscular endurance, cardio respiratory endurance, flexibility, and body composition. They also learned how to develop a fitness plan for their soldiers.

The firsties (seniors) were required to take a lifetime sport as their final experience. Their options included: Advanced Close Quarters Combat, Combatives Instructor Certification (Level I), Aerobic Fitness, Basketball, Cycling, Emergency Water Safety, Exercise Leadership, Golf, Ice Skating, Judo, Pickleball[28], Racquetball, Rock Climbing, SCUBA, Alpine Skiing, Cross Country Skiing, Soccer, Sport Physiology, Strength Development, Tennis, and Volleyball. In the sports courses, the cadets learned about the game. They were tested on the rules as well as officiating. It's commonplace for a young Army officer to be in charge of various sports in their unit; therefore, learning about sports had numerous advantages.

Fitness testing was another large component of the physical program. One of the fitness tests the cadets took was the Army Physical Fitness Test (APFT). Within the first three or four days after reporting to USMA, the new cadets would take the APFT, which is a three-event test composed of two minutes of push-ups, two minutes of sit-ups and a timed two-mile run. The cadets took this test twice

---

[27] Long ago, cadets at West Point did not leave the Academy for any vacations until the completion of their sophomore year. When they returned and were walking up the hill from the docks, they looked like a herd of cows coming home.

[28] Pickleball is a game played on a badminton court with the net at 34" at the center. The equipment consists of a perforated plastic baseball-sized ball and paddles.

each year and will continue to take it semi-annually throughout their years as Army officers.

SOME THINGS YOU DON'T CHANGE

There was and still is one fitness test administered by DPE that puts fear into the hearts of the cadets: the Indoor Obstacle Course Test (IOCT). The IOCT has been a part of the physical education curriculum since the 1940s. This eleven-event test challenges the cadets in muscular strength, muscular endurance, flexibility, agility, coordination, and anaerobic conditioning. It is made more challenging by it being a timed test, and usually there are several hundred cadets along with the staff and faculty watching and cheering. There is nothing quite like watching this test, and when someone sees it for the first time, s/he is absolutely amazed.

The IOCT was the one item in the curriculum that I knew I could never eliminate, and it has gone relatively unchanged for decades. It is, in my opinion, one of the few events that the graduates across decades have in common. Whenever I am around USMA grads, I always have to mention the IOCT, and there are always groans. However, there is also a great deal of animated conversation about the times they took the IOCT as cadets, and frankly a lot of pride in having completed it.

The IOCT is conducted in a very old gymnasium, Hayes Gym, which has an elevated running track. The gym is stuffy, hot, and the dust rises when the cadets take the test. Some cadets get a cough after the test, no doubt because the gym is old, ventilation is poor, and it is dry. The cadets refer to this persistent cough as the 'IOCT hack.' It is also common to see cadets vomit after the test. Courtesy of DPE, large yellow industrial trashcans are strategically placed at the finish line. Cadets have actually accused DPE of turning up the heat and pumping in dust when they take the test. I have always assured them that they are sucking the same dust that General Eisenhower inhaled!

A complete description and illustration of this amazing eleven-event fitness test and a diagram of the IOCT are at Appendix B. I included the IOCT diagram because USMA grads would be disappointed if I didn't.

CHAPTER SEVEN

WHAT IS A LEADERSHIP PHILOSOPHY?

A s I mentioned earlier, I wrote a leadership philosophy that I used as the Master of the Sword.

Leadership – "a process of influencing people by providing purpose, direction, and motivation to accomplish the mission and improve the organization."[29]

Philosophy – "the rational investigation of the truths and principles of being, knowledge or conduct…a system of principles for guidance in practical affairs."[30]

This definition of leadership is taken from Army doctrine. There are numerous definitions of leadership, but the definition in ADP 6-22 takes it a step farther with the verb "improve," which ultimately is all about making the organization a better place. It fundamentally addresses the importance of stewardship, which includes developing other leaders.

---

[29] ADP 6-22 Army Leadership August, 2012, p. 1.
[30] Robert B. Costello, ed., Random House Webster's College Dictionary. (New York: Random House, 1992), 1014.

It is important that Army leaders also strive to improve everything entrusted to them including their people, facilities, equipment, training, and resources. Imagine what organizations would be like if *everyone* in the organization worked on improving the organization and acting as stewards for the present and the future.

On 24 June 1997, the first day I walked into DPE as the Master of the Sword, I was known by most of the members of the department because I had only been gone for ten months. But there was a big difference. Now, I was the appointed leader. I was in charge!

While I was known in the department, I had to make sure they clearly understood how I was going to lead. My leadership philosophy helped a great deal. It described how I intended to lead, what folks could expect of me, and what I expected of others. It became my promise; a handshake with the organization.

The first time I met with the faculty, I not only went over my leadership philosophy, I gave a copy to each member of the department. Additionally, when new members arrived in the department, we had an office call, and I went over my leadership philosophy with them. This served as a great centerpiece to have a conversation around after the initial background questions. It helped provide the context for how we would work together, and it laid out my leadership point of view. My leadership philosophy guided me well during my seven-year journey as the Master of the Sword. The tenets of my leadership philosophy — care, dignity and respect, development, managing change, diversity, pride, maintaining a sense of humor, and wellness — follow.

CARE

I worked for an officer who was a big bear of a man with a wonderful charismatic personality. Revising the Theodore Roosevelt quote by replacing the word 'people' with 'soldier' he would say, "Soldiers don't care how much you know until they know how much you care."

There was a reason that this was the first tenet of my leadership philosophy. I believed that if you took care of people, if they felt appreciated for what they did, and respected for who they were, they would do their jobs well and be fully engaged at work. And frankly, it was simply the right thing to do.

Care was divided into three areas: family, cadets, and staff and faculty. The Army, not unlike the business world, is a fast-paced, very busy environment. If we were not careful, we could overlook and neglect those closest to us, our family. There were a lot of opportunities to volunteer at USMA, and for some, it was similar to being like a kid in a candy shop.

The favorite for some was the chance to work with a sports team. Very often, former members of teams returned to the faculty and worked with the team as an Officer Representative (OR). The role of the OR was very broad. They mentored the cadets, monitored grades, attended practices, and traveled with the team. And, frankly, because cadets were a lot of fun to be around, it was not hard for one's volunteering to take up an enormous amount of time. The result was that an assignment that could potentially be rich in quality family time became one focused on cadets and their development resulting in the neglect of developing a stronger family. It was the unintentional outcome of very good intentions.

I always sat down with my departing faculty to get their observations on their assignment in DPE. I would ask, "What is one piece of advice you would give to the new faculty?" Without hesitation one fine young officer said, "Tell them not to take on too many activities. Spend more time with their families." During his three-year tour[31]

---

[31] Army officers normally serve on the faculty for three years.

in DPE, this officer was an OR for the varsity swim team and club triathlon team, Bible study group leader, and he mentored a large number of cadets. He spent many evenings and weekends away from his family working with cadets.

Caring for cadets is very important. At USMA, cadets were cared for both in and out of the classroom. In the classroom, if a cadet was struggling, it was important to get to them quickly and understand what was going on. It was not unusual for cadets to be dealing with significant emotional issues in their lives. Sometimes, all you had to do was ask the question, "How are you doing?"

Shortly after the Christmas break, I was observing an instructor teach and noticed a cadet wearing his Gym Alpha[32] in a class when he should have been wearing his class uniform. I also noticed a large, greasy stain on the back of his t-shirt. After class I asked him if he was okay. He proceeded to tell me that during the holiday he had been in a severe car accident. This young man went into great detail about the accident and then almost without missing a beat he said, "And my mom was killed."

I was shocked that this young man had returned to school. We talked for a few more minutes, and I asked him if he was going to counseling. He said that he was and that his mom would have wanted him to return to school. As we finished the conversation he said, "Ma'am, thanks for talking to me." I spoke with the instructor, and fortunately he had also talked to this young man and knew what was going on in his life.

Care about co-workers must not be overlooked. I always spoke of DPE as a family, and I viewed myself as the head of the family. And, like any family, we dealt with a significant range of challenges on a

---

[32] Gym A is the uniform cadets wear when they work out; normally running shoes, white socks, shorts and a t-shirt. A running suit with a jacket and long pants are also part of this uniform.

regular basis. At any given time, we could have someone in the hospital, sick, injured, engaged, recently married, parenting a new baby, or dealing with a sick parent. These were recurring life challenges for sure, but if not effectively addressed, they could significantly impact the capacity for faculty members and staff to be effective at work. Leaders need to care about everyone, all the time.

I would always visit a faculty or family member if s/he were in the hospital. As you can imagine, in DPE the faculty was extremely physically active, so there were the occasional injuries. The visits wouldn't last long, especially if I were visiting a new mother.

Early on I decided to keep it simple, and I would always take the same gift. For my faculty, I took a PowerBar™ and a bottle of water. When visiting a new mom, that was easy – a box of chocolates. I would always remind them that chocolate has special healing properties. When a baby was born, I gave the classic children's book, *Goodnight Moon*, a favorite book of my children.

The department had a Cup and Flower Fund, a special fund in which all could contribute annually. These funds were used to send flowers or to purchase a small gift. A traditional Army gift for a new baby was a baby cup with the unit symbol engraved.

Unfortunately, I also attended funerals. I have had some tell me that it is too hard, that they couldn't go to a funeral or wake. It is not easy for me; I'm an emotional person, but it was always powerful. Very often, I would see a side of the individual that I had not had the opportunity to see before. I saw a gentleman who worked for me give the eulogy at his dad's funeral, which was very moving. At one graveside service, I had the honor of presenting the American flag to the wife of a department member. Her father had had a distinguished career in the U.S. Air Force. I always attended these services in my uniform. I believe that made it very visible to others at the wake or funeral that it was not only Maureen LeBoeuf who cared, but that the

Department of Physical Education and the United States Military Academy cared as well.

It was also important to celebrate! Each month, with a gentle reminder from my administrative assistant, I would write a birthday card to those having a birthday that month. It took very little time, and I always received a few 'thank yous' each month. In fact, some began to send *me* a birthday card. My administrative assistant was also great about baking a birthday cake for members of the Admin section, and I would be sure that we had a cake for her on her birthday.

Recognizing excellence plays an important role in an organization because it sends a strong message. I wanted to find a way to recognize members of the department when they did something above and beyond by giving them a small token. I had no money in the budget for such things, so we came up with the *Master of the Sword Bar*, which came to be known as the MOS Bar. It needed to be simple, and, because I had to purchase them, inexpensive. It was nothing more than a PowerBar™ with a customized wrapper developed by a member of the admin staff who was a genius with PowerPoint™.

At our monthly staff and faculty meeting, I would always begin by recognizing various accomplishments. The MOS bars were given out very sparingly, and everyone would cheer when one was awarded. We had fun with this. After a semi-annual physical fitness test, which included a timed two-mile run, I awarded several mini-MOS bars. These were the Hershey™ miniature candy bars with a miniaturized custom wrapper. These went to the individuals who passed me during the run!

A cadet called me one afternoon and asked me if I actually had MOS Bars. I told her yes, and she then asked if I would present some to members of her regiment who had achieved physical excellence. I attended lunch formation and presented the MOS bars to a few deserving cadets to the cheers of a thousand cadets. Great fun!

The DPE children had a special place in my heart. I have seen many born and grow up over the years they spent at West Point. We had promotion and award ceremonies in the department, and the families were always invited. I would get up and talk about the individual who was being recognized and then pin on his or her new rank or award. Very often the young children would watch, and I wanted to get them more involved in the ceremony. My administrative assistant located a ribbon, a very simple blue ribbon with the words 'Proud to be a Military Kid' in gold letters. These children would stand proudly when I presented their special ribbon. I know that the parents appreciated the special recognition of their children.

Leaders need to write notes. The act of note writing does not take a great deal of time, can have significant positive impact, but does require discipline. If a note is to have the intended impact, the discipline to get the note written in a timely manner and sent to the recipient is imperative. Sending an e-mail of thanks or a text with a thumbs up emoji has its place, but there is nothing like a hand-written note.

Unfortunately, note writing has become a lost art, despite the fact that it simply requires some time, good stationery and the discipline to get it done. If you don't currently write notes, start. Who is that person in your work or personal life who might need a few words of thanks or encouragement?

When our son Jay started Cadet Basic Training at West Point, Joe would send him a note each day. These were short notes of encouragement written on 3x5 cards. *Stay positive! Another day done! Be a good member of your squad.* You get the idea, little inspirational words for when times got tough. These notes also served as a reminder that Joe was thinking about him.

We hosted a party for Jay to celebrate his graduation from USMA. He was making a few remarks and thanking various individuals who had assisted him along the way. He then called Joe up and he pulled out all of the 3x5 cards he had written to him during CBT four years earlier. The cards were dog eared and held together with a butterfly clip. Jay said he had carried those cards with him during his cadet career. Those short notes served as a source of inspiration and strength for Jay during his, at times, bumpy journey as a cadet.

I have a friend who was diagnosed with breast cancer and had to undergo twenty-five days of radiation. I went to the local craft store and purchased blank note cards with envelopes. The cards and envelopes were pink. I purchased several embellishments and stickers to decorate the cards. Next, I found inspirational quotes, prayers and words that I printed out and pasted into each of the cards. I numbered the envelopes 1 to 25 and placed a card inside each one. I stacked the cards and tied them together with ribbon and a bow. I gave them to my friend and suggested that she open one envelope each day. She was both surprised and touched. At the conclusion of her treatment she told me that she looked forward to opening a card each day after her treatment, and especially on the last day because written inside was, *You're done!*

As I mentioned earlier, sending notes and letters can be very impactful in showing someone that you care. Another benefit is they serve as great reminders of beloved friends and family and time you spent together. Jackie and I have a special notebook in which we write notes to each other. On the cover we wrote, 'Dear Mommy – Dear Jackie.' When I started the notebook, it was to assist Jackie with her writing, and it also provided a different way for her to communicate with me, specifically in a case when she didn't want to tell me something to my face. There are some sweet notes in that notebook, and I'm so happy to have it.

Even the smallest of notes can go a long way. I'd include notes in Jay and Jackie's school lunches quite often. *Good luck on your math test! Learn something new today! Have a good lax practice! Enjoy your pb+j!* Or a simple, *I love you!*

A few years ago, I sat down at my home computer and there was a sticky note on my monitor with 'Mom I love you!' That simple note is still on my computer. Another time when Jackie was a little girl and had gotten into trouble, she slid a note under the door with an apology and a Hershey Kiss (nice touch) taped to the note. She learned the importance of note writing at an early age.

Sending a note when there is sadness or a tragedy in someone's life is also extremely important. People will often comment, 'I don't know what to say.' That is a weak excuse, since there are cards for everything these days, and you can find an appropriate card and pen a few lines. It's not about the words; it is about showing you are thinking about the individual during a challenging time in their life.

I had a leader tell me that she knows, at times, the individuals who work for her are required to put in long hours. She'll often send a personal note to a worker's family thanking them for the sacrifice they are making and letting them know what a great job their family member is doing. With the note she'll also include a gift card to a local restaurant. I think this is a terrific idea that no doubt is well received.

Leaders must also have good stationery. In the military, general officers have special stationery. There is a red flag at the top of the stationery with one to four stars depending on the rank of the general officer. These are referred to as star notes, and it was not unusual when walking around to see star notes posted in the work space of a recipient. Can you imagine sending a note to someone and they actually put it on their bulletin board?

Caring doesn't take any special training, but you must be sincere. People know immediately if what you are doing is merely a chore and not from the heart. Look around and figure out what you can do to show that you truly care.

Takeaways Regarding Care

- Care about those who work with and for you.
- Ask the question – 'How are you doing?' Listen. Care about the answer!
- Write birthday cards.
- Make hospital visits.
- Attend wakes and funerals.
- Send notes.
- Be sincere!

DIGNITY AND RESPECT

There is a term that used to be common at the military academy: hazing. Hazing was an abuse of power and very often used to denigrate an individual. I am pleased to report that hazing is no longer tolerated at USMA. However, the cadets often referred to DPE as 'a haze.' Very often when talking with cadets, I would ask them what they thought of DPE, and the response would be 'DPE is a haze.'

I would probe. "Who taught you plebe swimming?"

The cadet would give me the name of their instructor. "Mr. McVan was my instructor."

I would ask, "Was Mr. McVan a good instructor?"

"Mr. McVan was awesome!" I would continue to ask the same questions about other courses they took, and the answers were almost always positive. I would then ask, "So how exactly is DPE a haze?"

The response, "Ma'am, you know what we mean."

I would say to the cadets, "If you think that, because we hold you to high standards, and you refer to that as we are being a haze, then that is fine." Having and enforcing high standards are what I expected. However, I would not condone giving cadets a hard time simply because they are cadets.

There was a time when the members of the faculty did, in fact, haze cadets. It was common to see a cadet being yelled at in front of his/her classmates – a humiliating practice and one that is not acceptable. In fact, when I in-briefed the Army officers who had graduated from USMA, I would tell them that regardless of how the faculty had treated them or what they had observed when they were cadets, I would not tolerate any abuse of cadets. On occasion it was necessary to correct someone, but it was done behind closed doors.

Our subordinates are always watching. Over time, they will begin to model our behavior, good or bad. Very often it is because they admire and respect the boss, and figure if the boss acts in that manner and has been successful, then the behavior must work. Treating people well is important at all levels, but it becomes even more important as someone is promoted because with a promotion comes more power and influence. It is important not to abuse and misuse that power.

Dignity and respect are easy, nothing more than the 'Platinum Rule,' treat others the way they want to be treated.

Key Takeaways Regarding Dignity and Respect

- Treat everyone well.
- Don't tolerate abuse or misuse of power.
- Model the behavior you expect from those around you.

Development

Similar to other organizations, DPE was a very busy place to work. Often, an instructor arrived at work at 6:30 a.m. and left for the day at 6:30 p.m. The idea of professional development was one more task to add to an already full plate. In order to truly be a learning organization, we had to plan for and implement a professional development program.

There were several ways that we worked to incorporate professional development into the academic year. We would start the year with an off-site program. The venue changed each year, but the primary focus always centered on teaching. These programs gave different members of the faculty an opportunity to present on various topics relevant to teaching. It also served as a way to underscore that teaching was our number one priority. During these offsites, we also used the time together for some team-building activities. Each year, approximately one-third of the Army officers rotated out, and we received six to eight new instructors. A 30+% turnover for any organization is not trivial and can be disruptive. Participating in sporting activities allowed the new members to quickly assimilate into the department, and it also gave them an opportunity to 'show off' their particular talents.

A professional development theme was selected each year, allowing for good planning and continuity. During our staff and faculty meetings, in addition to the regular business, there was a well-planned and executed professional development session. One year the theme was 'Army 101.' This may sound strange. However, it became apparent that while we were teaching at the United States Military Academy, many of our civilians did not have a true understanding of the structure and mission of the U.S. Army. The Army officers would get up and give a tutorial on their specific branch and its overall role and function in the Army. This was extremely effective and gave the officers a chance to showcase their branch. The result was that the civilians commented that they learned a lot about the Army and the role of our graduates as officers.

Reading about our profession was also required. The Chief of Staff of the Army developed and implemented a professional reading program for the Army.

I had several copies of each book purchased and placed in a central location so members of the department had easy access.

Part of our professional development program included attending briefings and lectures. Occasionally, we were fortunate to have a guest speaker in our department. On two occasions, General (Retired) Barry McCaffrey[33] came to the department to speak. This eloquent soldier and scholar shared his insights on the drug situation in the United States and the war in Iraq. Colonel (Retired) Don Snider, an expert on the Army profession and a talented member of the USMA faculty in the Department of Social Sciences, also spoke. Every organization has individuals with a wide range of experience who can be called upon to help other parts of the organization develop professionally.

Reflection was something that we talked about a lot in the department. Reflection is one of the fundamental elements of effective leader development programming. For example, the faculty was encouraged to think about how a class was conducted. What worked? What didn't? How can I teach the lesson better the next time? How might I share a strategy that worked rather well? In our busy, hectic lives, we don't always take the time to reflect.

---

[33] General (Retired) Barry McCaffrey retired from the Army as the most highly decorated four-star general in the U.S. Army; he served from 1996-2001 as a member of the President's Cabinet and the National Security Council for drug-related issues. He served as the Bradley Distinguished Professor of International Studies at the United States Military Academy.

As an aid to assist my faculty members in reflection, one year I gave each of them a classic black and white composition notebook and two brand-new #2 pencils, sharpened. One faculty member was concerned that I was going to check their notebooks. I honestly didn't think this would be helpful; I believe reflection is a private matter. However, during routine counseling sessions, some would bring their notebook and would share some of their reflections with me.

One can grow both personally and professionally if some time is spent reflecting on a regular basis. Sometimes what we taught was not always what was written as a part of a lesson plan. The following is what I wrote in my teaching journal on 21 September 2001:

"Ten days ago terrorists attacked the United States. I stood in horror as I watched the World Trade Towers collapse to the ground. Overwhelming grief consumed me…I had to leave the DPE projection room because I thought I would break down. I knew I had just witnessed live, the deaths of thousands of people. Today the count exceeds 6400!!! Last night President George W. Bush declared WAR on terrorism. I'm not sure any of us truly understand just what kind of war this will be.

During the last ten days I have had trouble concentrating and being focused on teaching. I did however spend a couple of class periods allowing my cadets (18 men, all yearlings) to talk about the attack on the U.S. These young men will go into an Army that is at war!!!"

~ M. LeBoeuf, personal teaching journal

In DPE the faculty did not only teach. Every member of the faculty had what I would refer to as a major additional duty. For example, there was an operations officer, human resources officer, logistics officer, and facilities scheduling officer, to name a few. I encouraged members of the department to learn what others did outside of the classroom. Many had functions that required working closely with each other, creating a coherence essential to effective departmental operations. I believed if they better understood what others did, it would give them an appreciation for the work of other members of the department as well as a better understanding of the department.

Visiting other Army units was also encouraged, especially for the civilian faculty. For some, the only Army installation they had been on was West Point. As great as West Point is, there is nothing like being on a post with soldiers in tactical units. The first opportunity for our civilians to go to an Army post was at Fort Drum, the home of the 10th Mountain Division, in Watertown, New York. They did not merely observe, the commanders let them fully participate in training with the soldiers.

One senior civilian faculty member returned from the experience with a great story. He said the commander had given them several options for training events they could participate in with the soldiers. The event he selected was a road march; he said he thought it would be like going for a hike. He was given a backpack to wear with fifty pounds of Army manuals to simulate the load the soldiers would be carrying. They wanted to make sure he had the 'real experience.' The road march began. Shortly after they started, someone yelled, *"Incoming!"*

The senior civilian faculty member said all of a sudden, soldiers were running and throwing themselves to the ground. His 'hike' quickly turned into a very tough physical event, and he loved it! When they returned, the excitement was palpable. It was great to hear them talk about their experiences. A real highlight was that it also gave them the opportunity to see and catch up with the officers they had taught as cadets.

We can also learn from others who share the same passion for the profession. At the United States Military Academy, we looked to our friends at the other service academies. The missions are very similar: We all want to produce the most physically fit officer (Army, Navy, Air Force or Marine) possible in the four years they are cadets or midshipmen. Within the first few months of becoming the Master of the Sword, I traveled to the Air Force Academy and the Naval Academy to meet my counterparts. In an effort to continue those conversations, we began the All Academy Physical Development Symposium.

The Academies and other colleges and universities with strong military programs such as North Georgia College, the Citadel, and Virginia Military Institute as well as the Army Fitness School, were also invited. This forum took place every other year at West Point, the Naval Academy in Annapolis, or the Air Force Academy in Colorado Springs. Faculty members from the academies gave talks on relevant topics. Additionally, those who have similar positions, such as oversight of the intramural program or fitness testing, had an opportunity to meet and discuss best practices. We learned a lot from each other, and some great friendships were formed.

Professional development is extremely important for an organization if it is to stay relevant and move forward. Publishing in professional journals and trade magazines, attending conferences, reading about your profession, and bringing in experts to present lectures are all ways in which members of an organization can grow and develop. It is important for the leader of the organization to engage in these activities as well.

Each year several members of the department would present at our professional conferences such as: the New York State Alliance for Health, Physical Education, Recreation and Dance (NYSAHPERD), and the national association, American Alliance for Health, Physical Education, Recreation and Dance (AAHPERD) for the physical education profession. I always made an effort to attend and, if possible, to present. The DPE faculty was extremely talented, and their presentations were always excellent and well attended.

When it became a requirement for the faculty to present and publish, some who had been in the department for years were very resistant. One of my senior civilian faculty members was one such individual, a tough character who was never lacking for an opinion. He was truly a subject-matter expert in rock climbing and downhill skiing, and I thought he had a lot to share. He absolutely did not want to write for journals or present at conferences, though, and in a hallway conversation, he began to question me on the value of writing and presenting.

He was one of the individuals who had gone through the RIF process and had to become an assistant coach. He also was affected by the requirement to move out of government housing. Quite simply, he was not happy with all of the changes, and writing and publishing was another major change. I asked him if he thought he was truly a subject-matter expert in downhill skiing and rock climbing; he responded that he was. I then told him that I thought he had a responsibility to share his knowledge outside the walls of USMA. He said that he had never thought of it that way. I am pleased to report that he has published and has presented at the state and national level, and he has served as a consultant to other colleges and universities who have incorporated rock climbing into their programs.

During my tenure with DPE, we began a rather ambitious project of writing a book. One of my civilian professors and I served as the editors. The book was designed as a comprehensive resource for ideas, recommendations, and best practices for physical educators from elementary thorough the college years. The book, *Fit & Active: The West Point Physical Development Program*, was published in 2008. It was a fascinating project with twenty-eight members of the department serving as contributors to the book.

Any organization can benefit from a professional development program. If individuals and organizations want to remain vital and relevant, then education and training are the keys. However, it is imperative that the leadership in the organization fully engages in and supports the professional development programs.

Key Takeaways Regarding Development

- Learn about your profession.
  - ◆ Attend & present at conferences.
  - ◆ Publish in your discipline.
- Read books that will help you grow.
- Reflect.
- Talk to others in your profession.
- Provide the resources for members of the organization to grow in their profession.

MANAGING CHANGE

I'm sure by now most everyone has heard about or read the book, *Who Moved My Cheese?*, authored by Spencer Johnson. Prior to my arrival in 1994 as the Director of Instruction, the 'cheese' in the department had definitely been moved! I knew that dealing with change had to be part of my leadership philosophy. We needed to be adaptive and flexible in our behavior.

At the War College, we were taught an acronym, VUCA, which stands for:

Volatile
Uncertain
Complex
Ambiguous

Certainly, this acronym can be applied to most organizations today. In my leadership philosophy, I focused on two major changes that were occurring in the department: the renovation of our building and a significant change in the curriculum.

Arvin Cadet Physical Development Center (CPDC) was the building where the majority of all physical education classes were taught and where the offices are located. Today, it is a large facility with over 500,000 square feet. Initially, it consisted of six different structures built over a seventy-year period; twenty-seven roof levels; numerous mechanical rooms; and three pools. Arvin CPDC had a number of issues, including poor traffic circulation, life safety, gender equity, and mechanical systems that were old and not integrated.

This was not a minor renovation; the majority of the building was demolished. The project was awarded in May 1999 with demolition complete in December 2001. When the major demolition/renovation began, the department had to move out and began teaching activity classes all over West Point. Being flexible and having a good attitude were key. For example, the faculty had to learn where the classrooms were and had to adjust the class schedules since cadets were now required to travel farther distances to get to class. Classes were forced to start a few minutes late, and the cadets were to be dismissed a few minutes early.

The USMA classes of 2003 and 2004 did not have a good usable fitness facility during their entire four years as cadets. During the summer when the new cadets[34] were participating in Cadet Basic Training, I would make it a point to go out and talk to them about the importance of physical fitness and excellence in the physical program. It gave me an opportunity to tell them about the status of the building and to promise them a first-class physical education experience.

Events leading up to the actual renovation of Arvin CPDC were interesting and significantly instructive for me. It was my first exposure to the political process involved with military construction

---

[34] New cadets – the rising freshman. This term is used to identify the cadets before they are accepted into the Corps of Cadets which occurs upon successful completion of Cadet Basic Training just prior to the start of the academic year.

and not one that I would like to repeat. I saw first-hand how a single, powerful politician could stop a project from moving forward. It was unfortunate because these politics delayed the renovation for well over a year. The building that was at ninety-five percent design had to be redesigned because a politician argued that the building was too big, and a redesign would save the taxpayers a lot of money. The bottom line was it did not save the taxpayers a dime. In fact, when the building was completed in the spring of 2005, it was smaller than the original design and carried a higher price tag. This was all as a result of the personal issues and preferences of one individual, not grounded in facts associated with the design.

The curriculum had also changed, so it was important for the faculty to not only be aware of the changes, but to understand why the changes were being made. Some curricular changes were significant, one of which was a review of the gymnastics curriculum. My effort to have this course changed is an excellent example of truly how resistant to change some can be.

Gymnastics had been taught at USMA since 1838 when a horizontal bar was installed in an academic building.[35] Gymnastics is a course steeped in a lot of tradition with, at the time, too many gender specific tasks. It is a course in the core curriculum that I believed needed to be changed and brought into the 21st Century, making it more appropriate to Army needs.

During CBT, the men and women cadets did everything together. However, in gymnastics, they were put into separate lines. The male cadets would get in one line, the women cadets in another. Even the grading cards were different. The men's were white and the women's were a salmon color. Not pink, but close.

The men would do gymnastics events that were typical Olympic male events: parallel bars, horizontal bar and rings. The women would

---

[35] Degen, R. (1968). p. 26.

work on the uneven bars, balance beam and floor exercise. This always bothered me, because in all of my years in the Army, whenever I attended training, this was never done. I felt strongly that we were sending the wrong message to the cadets. I was confident that we could come up with events that had more of a military appropriate focus and less of an Olympic gymnastics, gender-based perspective.

At the start of the academic year in 1999, I selected a committee to review the gymnastics curriculum and develop new lessons for the course. I had not required that the chair of the committee give me regularly scheduled briefings to update me on the progress. I later realized that this was a big mistake on my part. After several months of work, I was to receive the report on the changes to the curriculum.

The night before the committee was going to brief me, our Visiting Professor came in to see me. He said, "Maureen, you are not going to see what you want tomorrow at the briefing." He went on to explain that the committee had not changed anything; they simply validated that what they were teaching was correct and the right skills were being taught. I very much appreciated him telling me this information because it gave me some time to think about what I had done wrong. It was obvious to me that I failed to effectively communicate to the committee my intent that I expected the course to change.

The next day I went into the briefing, and the information I had received the day prior was correct, they had not changed a thing. I could have gotten very angry and told them to start over, but I decided I would wait. Wait I did, for about two years, until one afternoon I was talking with a member of the gymnastics committee. We were standing in Hayes Gymnasium watching class, and he said, "I can't continue to teach gymnastics if it doesn't change."

He was one of the instructors in the department that, when the Ph.D. requirement was mandated, he enrolled in a program and earned a doctorate. I honestly saw a difference in the faculty who had earned their doctorates. They brought a new energy and enthusiasm to their teaching; they no longer wanted to operate the way they had been for decades. When he told me he wanted the course to change, I knew I had the person who could help make change happen. He became a member of what Kotter, in his book, *Leading Change*, refers to as a guiding coalition, an essential step in any change process.

Once again, I stood up a committee to review the Gymnastics curriculum. I gave guidance in writing with scheduled in-process reviews (IPR) with both the head of the committee and with the full committee. At my first IPR with the committee, a chart was displayed that indicated all of the goals and objectives that were being accomplished by the course. This time I did get angry and told them that whoever had made the chart had wasted his time. They had my guidance, and the course was going to change!

At subsequent IPRs, members of the committee talked about a pilot study they had conducted for a couple of new lessons. Instead of wearing shorts, t-shirt and sneakers to class, the cadets wore their battle dress uniforms (BDUs), boots, and load-bearing equipment. They noted two things, the HOOAH[36] factor was increased during class, and it was more difficult for the cadets to climb ropes in boots. I saw both of these as extremely positive. The cadets were motivated, and it was harder to climb in boots. Motivation is always a good thing when trying to teach a new task or skill. Discovering that it is

---

[36] hooah (hoo ah) adj., adv., n., v., conj., interj., excla. [Orig. unknown] Slang. 1. Referring to or meaning anything and everything except "no". 2. What to say when at a loss for words. 3.a. Good copy. b. Roger. c. Solid copy. d. Good. e. Great. f. Message received. g. Understood. h. Acknowledged. 4.a. Glad to meet you. b. Welcome. 5. "All right!" 6.a. I don't know the answer, but I'll check on it. b. I haven't the foggiest idea. 7. I am not listening. 8. "That is enough of your drivel; sit down!" 9. Yes. 10. "You've got to be kidding me!" 11. Thank you. 12. Go to the next slide. 13. You've taken the correct action. 14. I don't know what that means, but I'm too embarrassed to ask for clarification. 15. Squared away (S/he's pretty hooah.) 16. Amen!

more difficult to climb ropes in boots was important because soldiers normally wear their boots when climbing ropes.

At the conclusion of the committee's work, several course changes were made. The name of the course also changed from Gymnastics to Military Movement. Cadets still referred to the course as gymnastics, but the content of the course had changed, for the good. I did not get all of the changes I wanted for the course, so there was a compromise on both sides. It was a win-win.

The instructor I had the conversation with that day became the new course director for the Military Movement course, and he developed two new lessons that incorporated the new rock-climbing wall. Imagine the enthusiasm of the cadets today when they go to class in BDUs and learn how to move over rock. Sounds exactly like the type of skill our soldiers need!

Change is not easy for any organization, and it is made even more difficult when the organization is rich in history and has not changed in a long, long time. As a leader, you must work with the members of your organization to move them toward change. It is a process, and it takes time. Be patient, but be persistent!

Key Takeaways Regarding Managing Change

- Be flexible; change is inevitable.
- Have key members of the organization assist with the change.
- Stand up a committee.
- Put guidance for change in writing.
- Have regularly-scheduled meetings to check progress.
- Brief everyone on the change.
- Implement the change.
- Focus on the future.

Diversity

Diversity may have a different meaning to everyone. For me, I looked at diversity beyond the obvious of gender, race, religion, or ethnicity. It also included military, civilian, where people grew up, where they have been stationed, branches, levels in the Army, where they worked, experience in higher education, and deployment to combat.

When I was a young instructor in DPE in the mid-80s, I had a senior faculty member refer to me as a *rookie*. I thought, I may be a first-year instructor, but I'm not a rookie. I had been in the Army for ten years, had assignments at various levels in the United States and in Germany, was a helicopter pilot, and had undergraduate and graduate degrees in education. While I was a new instructor and certainly had a lot to learn, I was not a rookie as a military professional. I did not believe that that particular senior faculty member valued the talents that I brought to the department. His behavior lacked an attitude of truly understanding diversity.

I wanted the military faculty to value the civilian faculty, and I also wanted the civilians to value the military faculty. At West Point, the military/civilian faculty is referred to as *a blend of excellence*. However, sometimes their differences can be a source of tension, which I worked hard to diminish. I always told the officers that they could learn a great deal from the civilian faculty, as many are truly subject matter experts. I also reminded the civilian faculty that these young officers had a lot of experience, some had even served in combat, and that they could learn from them as well.

Mentoring was a method that we used to try to break down any barriers to inclusion. This began before the military faculty arrives in DPE. Once selected to teach at USMA, an officer was sent to earn a graduate degree. The communication between DPE and the officers began while they were in grad school. Information about the department and what courses they will teach was sent in order to help them structure their curricular choices and prepare for their arrival. It was a civilian who mentored the officer while still in school. More importantly, the mentor was a friendly face for the officer upon arrival in the department and an essential aspect of the on-boarding process. This was one way in which we ensured that there was one civilian the Army officer knew before arriving in the department. Many civilians continued this mentoring after the officer arrived; they would observe teaching or would simply serve as a sounding board.

The civilian faculty in DPE still has a long and distinguished history. Most familiar is Marty Maher, a colorful Irish immigrant who became known outside the gates of USMA when Tyrone Powers portrayed him in the 1955 movie, *The Long Gray Line*. The contributions of those who have served are remembered long after their departure. There is a wall in the department with pictures of former members of the civilian faculty. The placard above the pictures reads, 'Distinguished Educators.'

In the Army, we were required to attend certain annual trainings, and one such topic discussed was sexual harassment. We had an officer who had an additional duty as the Equal Opportunity Officer and was required to give an informational briefing on sexual harassment. On one such occasion, the department was gathered, and the instructor began with a joke. He said, "I found this joke off of the internet." I thought this might not be good. He went on to tell the joke and I was right – it was totally inappropriate.

Fortunately, when he got to the punch line, there was not a single snicker. There was absolute silence. He had a rather perplexed look on his face, the 'Don't you get it?' kind of look. He then went on with his class. I sat there and knew that I could not leave the room without getting up and making a comment. When the session was over,

I stood up and said, "I'm sure that CPT Whitaker[37] didn't intend to tell the joke that he told, because it was inappropriate." He gave me a look of total confusion.

About one second after I dismissed the department, the deputy, and a tough no-nonsense kind of guy, had this officer in his office for a serious one-way counseling session. At the same time, the officer's office mate, a woman, came to see me. She assured me that he would never knowingly tell an off-color joke. She was shocked that he told such a joke and was convinced he didn't understand the joke and the implications of telling it.

The joke teller had an office call with me as well. He stood in front of my desk and told me he had interpreted the joke differently. While this may seem unbelievable, I honestly think he didn't understand the joke. I scheduled a department meeting the next day. At the meeting, CPT Whitaker apologized to the department for the inappropriate joke. It was a good lesson for all.

If you truly embrace diversity and inclusion, then you don't tell jokes that may disparage another group, and the internet might not be the best source for humor! After the apology, I received an e-mail from a new civilian faculty member. He essentially wrote that he was impressed to see how the situation had been handled in the department, and he was proud to be a member of an organization with such high standards and values.

As a part of our professional development program, I brought in a fellow department head, Colonel Andre Sayles. In addition to chairing the department of Electrical Engineering and Computer Science, Andre had also done some great work on diversity and inclusion, and he was a recognized Army expert, having done a great deal of research and writing on diversity as a student at the Army War College. I invited him to the department on a couple of occasions to

---

[37] Not his real name.

share information about this topic. It was always an inspiring session because he challenged us to think differently about diversity, which created the opportunity for great discussion and had significant positive impact on enabling our department's point of view on diversity and inclusion.

Andre described diversity as a process having three levels: accept differences, understand differences, and value differences. It is not that difficult for individuals to accept that someone is different. The next level is truly understanding the differences, which can be more challenging for some. Understanding does not always come quickly. Education is very important in order to have individuals move toward the true understanding and valuing of differences. Diversity education must be an ongoing process. There are numerous ways to conduct a diversity education program: guest speakers, special dinners with ethnic foods, and events that focus on the unique aspects of a culture.

Very often people will wonder why certain members of a group congregate. For example, in 1979 when I was in flight school, there were only a few women in the program. As mentioned earlier, I was struggling with certain aspects of my flight training, and the men never seemed to have any problems – at least they never mentioned them to me. I invited the women in the other flight classes to my room for coffee and dessert. During the course of the evening, it became apparent that I wasn't the only one having difficulty in certain areas of flight school. We talked, stories about flight school were told, and many helpful tips were shared. This was the first time I realized that the men were probably having the same types of problems. They simply didn't share. We women at flight school continued to get together over the next several months and continued to socialize long after those of us who started these coffees had completed our flight training and departed.

Decades later when I was at the Army War College, there were 320 students and twenty-five were women, eight percent of the class. We were all members of nineteen-person seminars, and I was the only woman in my seminar group. The women would get together for coffee, lunch, or for an evening social. Usually when a group (three or four) of the women were talking, one of our male classmates would walk by and say, "What are you ladies doing, planning to take over?" Of course we were!

Actually, what was happening when we would gather was this: we were nurturing that side of us that is unique, being women. I always felt good after one of these events. Individuals need to be allowed to nurture the side of themselves that is different and celebrate their uniqueness. It does not mean individualism outweighs the needs of the overall unit, but there must be a balance. The result will be an individual who is a more productive member of the organization.

As a leader, it is important to listen to those around you because they will offer different ways to view a problem or situation. Whenever I was going to make a significant decision, I would talk with the members of the leader team. Often these discussions would provide different perspectives that enabled for me a more holistic view of the considerations that should inform any given decision. Sometimes it changed the way I viewed a situation, sometimes it didn't, but I listened.

I believe it is important to listen closely enough so you can hear the differences. When I made a decision, the faculty knew it had been discussed. Not all of my decisions were popular, but I was confident that, at the end of the day, the members of the department knew I had the best interests of the department at heart.

I did, however, expect that when I made a decision, the discussion would be over. A senior military member of DPE who became a trusted confidant of mine told me that once a decision is made, like it or not, he accepts it as though it was his own good idea. He took ownership. This is a wonderful approach to take towards a decision.

Paying attention to diversity has nothing to do with being politically correct and everything to do with accepting, understanding, and valuing differences. A leader who takes the time to embrace diversity as well as effective, relational listening, will enable a more effective and engaged organization.

Key Takeaways Regarding Diversity

- Pay attention to diversity.
- Surround yourself with those who think differently than you.
- A diverse group of individuals who respect each other can make an organization a powerful place to work.
- Respecting differences is key.
- Education plays an important role in understanding diversity. Bring in experts.
- Don't tolerate intolerance!
- Listen closely to hear the differences.
- Gather information before you make a decision.
- Make the decision.
- Inform the members of the organization of the decision – move out!

PRIDE

We all wore uniforms in DPE, not only the Army officers; the civilian faculty wore them as well. You may recall that during my first tour in DPE, I was shocked when I first saw the uniform that I was required to wear. The teaching uniform consisted of black coaching shorts (that were way too short) and a grey polyester shirt with an oversized, black collar; black cross trainer shoes, white athletic socks which were pulled up; and black, polyester trousers with a narrow white stripe that ran the length of each leg. The uniform had been around for a long time. In fact, there is a picture in the book of the faculty taken in 1937, and the men in the picture were wearing the same style of pants!

When I returned to the department in 1994, I approached the department chair about the possibility of changing the uniform. He thought the uniform was functional and didn't need to be changed. I decided that I would have a customized shirt made for my personal use. I sent Lands' End™ the DPE crest and colors, and for a nominal fee, a sample was returned. It looked great. I then purchased some polo shirts with the DPE crest. I would wear these shirts to DPE social functions and around West Point, and, of course, everyone wanted to know where I purchased the shirts. It didn't take long before several members of the department had ordered the shirts as well.

There are times as a member of an organization when you think, *If I'm ever in charge, this is something I will change.* The uniform was that *something* I wanted to change. When I returned as the Master of the Sword, one of my first tasks was to go about changing the uniform. We adopted a more updated look with materials that were durable, functional, and looked sharp. Because we were at USMA, the uniform standard within the department was very strict. We corrected cadets if they were not wearing their uniforms correctly, and we made sure our uniforms were serviceable and worn correctly as well. This was an area that was also addressed when a new civilian faculty member arrived, as many were not accustomed to wearing a uniform, much less wearing a uniform to a high standard. It was especially important because when we stepped outside of our building, everyone knew that we were from the Department of Physical Education.

The change in the uniform was about much more than simply putting the department in a uniform that was updated and more functional. The new uniform also indicated a change in the culture, and that new changes were on the horizon.

Another change in the culture was to engage in activities we had never done before. We developed a motto for the department. The entire department was queried for recommendations and suggestions. The motto that we agreed on was 'Set the Standard – Maintain the Standard.' And, we did exactly that on a daily basis. We demonstrated a high standard and then enforced a high standard. This motto was a great source of pride; it appeared on all briefing slides along with the department crest.

There was a common template used whenever someone was briefing inside or outside the department. In April 2001, we established The Center for Physical Development Excellence, a research center located within DPE, created as a center of innovation and advancement for our discipline. The first time the director of the center came in to brief me, he had a different template, one that was unique to the center. He was enthusiastic and proud of the center; however, I told him that the center was in DPE, and he was to use the DPE template. Was this a big deal? To some it wouldn't be. However, I do believe as a leader you need to be aware at times that parts of the organization may splinter off and become their own entity within the organization. I have seen this happen in other organizations, and it is not healthy. This may not have happened with the center, but I wanted to make sure it didn't happen in DPE.

The DPE newsletter also served as a source of pride for the department. We wrote and published the newsletter twice each year. I often commented that I was glad we didn't have to publish a daily newsletter. Prior to publishing the first edition, we decided the newsletter needed a name. We asked the members of the department for suggestions, and the one selected was perfect: *The DPE Standard*. I liked how it linked to the department's logo. The newsletter was sent to my fellow department heads, the Academy leadership, former members of the department, and some commanders in the Army. It was a great way to showcase all of the great work being done in DPE. And yes, it gave me the opportunity to brag a bit and toot DPE's horn.

The newsletter included the accomplishments of former members of the department. We had several general officers among our ranks who were performing quite well in our Army. I also wrote a short column, *The Colonel's Corner*. These were my musings about my view of life in DPE. As I look back and read these semi-annual newsletters, they serve as a wonderful historical record of the department.

Pride is important in any organization; people want to be proud to say where they work. Pride in the way you dress, your workspace, and quality of work are all ways in which you can demonstrate on a daily basis you are a proud professional.

Key Takeaways Regarding Pride

- Develop ways to make employees proud of where they work.
- Wear clothing with the company logo.
- If there is a uniform, have a standard, and enforce the standard.
- Require workspaces to be organized.
- Share accomplishments of employees outside of the organization.
- Publish a newsletter.

MAINTAIN A SENSE OF HUMOR

This may seem like an unusual tenet to have as a part of a leadership philosophy, but I believe having a sense of humor can help a leader. As the middle child of nine, I learned at a young age the importance of a sense of humor.

While at the University of Georgia, I took a graduate class that focused on culture. The professor had done research on humor between different cultures. Humor is indeed an interesting part of one's culture because something that might be considered funny in one culture may not be funny in another; it may even be offensive. During one lecture, she said there are five different types of people when it comes to humor: 1) the producer, 2) the reproducer, 3) the producer/reproducer, 4) the receiver, and 5) the 'I don't get it.'

The producer is someone who has a quick wit, sees the humor in events, and makes others laugh. The reproducer is the individual who can retell a great joke, and his/her timing is perfect. The producer/reproducer is the person who has a quick wit and also can retell a joke. The receiver is the person who enjoys a good joke, but never tells a joke. The 'I don't get it' individual doesn't tell jokes and doesn't get the jokes. S/he may, however, laugh, but s/he is also the one looking around.

I realized as I sat in class that there are all five types of people in my family! My dad was a great joke and storyteller; however, he was not a real producer of humor. Timer, Bob, and Kevin, my three brothers, are producers/reproducers because they all have a quick wit and can tell jokes. My sisters fall into each of the other categories, and because I want to ensure my survival in the family, I won't share who has which type. I would like to think that I have a dry sense of humor, a quick wit, and love to retell a great joke, so I consider myself a producer/reproducer like my brothers.

I have used humor fairly successfully during my lifetime, including during my Army career. There are times when it is simply easier to laugh. Humor can also be used to break a tense situation. Very often when I would start a meeting, I would tell a funny story. It tends to relax people.

I have heard laughing referred to as internal jogging, you just plain feel good after. However, if you are not funny, don't force it by trying to be funny. It won't work, and people will be laughing *at* you and not *with* you. Also, as with anything else, humor has its place. When used inappropriately, it can be a problem. Remember the incident at the start of the sexual harassment training?

Probably the most important aspect of humor is our ability to laugh at ourselves. I make it a point to try to laugh each day. It may be as simple as reading the comics. Laughing releases endorphins, which make us feel good, so go ahead and laugh.

Key Takeaways Regarding Maintaining a Sense of Humor

- Don't take yourself too seriously.
- Laugh daily.
- If you are not funny, don't force it.
- Make sure humor is appropriate.

WELLNESS

Wellness is an aspect of my leadership philosophy I added after a few years as the Master of the Sword. (Note, it is important to recognize that your leadership philosophy is a living document and ought to mature as your leadership matures.) It falls into the category of 'walking the talk.' We would teach cadets about the importance of work/life balance or wellness, and I wanted to make sure that as a faculty, we were doing what we told the cadets they should be doing.

I taught the wellness course to the yearlings (sophomores), and on the first day of class, I had the following words written in large letters on cardboard and hung around the room:

- **Spiritual** – "The sense that life is meaningful, that life has purpose…the ethics, values, and morals that guide us and give meaning and value to life."[38]
- **Physical** – "Physically fit; eat well; get enough sleep; don't engage in risky activities; get regular exams."[39]
- **Social** – "The ability to relate well to others in all aspects of our lives."[40]
- **Emotional** – "Understand your own feelings and accept limitations."[41]
- **Intellectual** – "A state in which your mind is engaged in lively interaction with the world around you."[42]
- **Environmental** – "Live in a clean and safe environment that is not detrimental to your health."[43]

After a brief discussion about the definition of each, I then asked the cadets to go to the word that represented an area in their life where they felt they were strongest. They would then share why they believed the word resonated. Next, I asked them to move to the word that represented an area in which they were weakest. Again, they had the opportunity to share why this was so.

The cadets had a project I assigned which lasted for the duration of the course. They were to identify a specific area of their life that they believed needed improvement, develop a plan, and then work to improve in that specific area of wellness. During the last two lessons, the cadets would get up and talk about what they did and whether they noticed a change. This was very powerful because the cadets

---

[38] Hoeger, W.K. & Hoeger, S.A. (2005). Lifetime Physical Fitness and Wellness: A Personalized Program, 8th edition: Thompson Wadsworth, Belmont, CA. p. 472.

[39] Ibid, p. 7.

[40] Ibid, p. 7.

[41] Ibid, p. 7.

[42] Ibid, p. 7.

[43] Ibid, p. 7.

would genuinely open up and share some very personal aspects of their lives. More importantly, the project created the conditions for some true behavioral change over time.

One young woman spoke about the fact that her grandmother had passed away a few months earlier. The family had a tradition of a spaghetti dinner on Friday nights. Her family lived close to the academy, and she was able to get home frequently for this special dinner. However, once her grandmother died, it became too painful for her to go home, and she had even stopped talking to her family. She stood in front of her classmates and began to cry. She missed her grandmother terribly. She had chosen the emotional aspect of wellness for her project. Through reflection, she realized her family was being shut out of her life. She had been struggling with her emotional wellness, and it was having a negative impact on her social wellness.

In an effort to begin to work on this, she had gone home the previous Friday for the spaghetti dinner. She was still hurting, but she had started to work through the pain. She began to realize her family would be able to help her as they all worked through the grieving process.

Another cadet said that several years prior, his sister was ill and needed a bone marrow transplant. The type matching was done on family members. He was a perfect match, and his bone marrow was used. Unfortunately, his sister did not survive. He said he became so angry with God that he quit practicing his religion and quit praying. Spiritual wellness was the area he decided to focus on during the course. He described it as a process. He began to talk to his mother about his faith, and she began sending him articles and books to read. One can only imagine how powerful it was for his mother when her son began talking to her about his faith as she helped him work on improving his spiritual wellness.

"Do I make a difference?" That was the statement made by one of the students, an Army football player. This young man said his days all seemed the same, day in and day out. He would get up, eat breakfast, attend classes, eat lunch, attend classes, go to football practice, eat dinner, study, and prepare for the next day. He would then get up and start it all over the next day. To him, his life as a cadet seemed a bit like the movie, *Groundhog Day*.

This young man began to take a few minutes and write a journal entry each evening before he went to bed. As a result of his daily reflections, he realized that while his activities during the day didn't change a great deal, he did have several interactions with different people throughout his day. Reflecting on the interactions he had with classmates, teammates, company mates, instructors, mentors, and coaches helped him learn he was making a difference.

These are only a few examples of topics the cadets shared with the class. Certainly, every topic a cadet focused on was not always profound; some were as simple as working on getting a few minutes more sleep each night. I began to feel that, as a faculty, we needed to set an example and develop our own wellness plans. I added this to my leadership philosophy and required the members of the department to develop a personal wellness plan. An example of an actual wellness plan is in Appendix C.

Not unlike reflection, when individuals wrote their wellness plans out, it created the conditions that enabled their thinking about the different aspects of wellness in their lives. As a result, many realized their lives were out of balance, and they began the work of putting emphasis on the areas they recognized that needed more attention.

We taught wellness to the cadets for several years and emphasized the importance of leaders paying attention to the wellness of their soldiers as a fundamental imperative. It was invigorating to have it reinforced when General (Retired) John M. Keane, then the Vice Chief of Staff of the Army, signed and had published the *Well-Being Strategic Plan* for the Army on 5 January 2001.

In the document, well-being was defined as:

"the personal — physical, material, mental, and spiritual — state of Soldiers [Active, Reserve, Retirees, Veterans], civilians, and their families that contributes to their preparedness to perform the Army's mission."[44]

The importance of well-being was stressed in an Army Regulation as being a commander's business. A commander must pay attention to the overall well-being of his or her soldiers because ultimately the way a soldier feels will have a significant impact on mission accomplishment.[45]

"Commanders and other leaders committed to the professional Army ethic promote a positive command environment. If leaders show loyalty to their Soldiers, the Army, and the Nation, they earn the loyalty of their Soldiers. If leaders consider their Soldiers' needs and care for their well-being, and if they demonstrate genuine concern, these leaders build a positive command climate."[46]

The yearlings were team leaders, and their teams consisted of one cadet each. They were put 'in charge' of a plebe. Teaching the cadets about wellness created an opportunity for me and other members of the faculty to actually see that our sophomores were developing as leaders and were paying attention to the wellness of their plebe. Only a few questions had to be asked: "How is your plebe doing?" "Is your plebe eating well?" "How is your plebe doing academically?" "How is your plebe adjusting to being a cadet?" Very often I would not call on a specific cadet, but simply throw the questions out there. It was

---

[44] Department of the Army, Well-Being Strategic Plan, January 5, 2001, p. 3.

[45] Ibid, p. 4.

[46] Ibid, p. 4.

interesting watching them while they thought about their plebes because it was obvious that some had no idea what was going on in the life of the cadet for whom they were responsible.

A cadet once told me that, during an inspection[47] of his plebe's room, he found several bottles of supplements. He asked the cadet why he had so many vitamins. The cadet said he was trying to lose weight; so instead of eating, he was taking vitamins. He talked with him about the importance of diet and eating right and made an appointment for his plebe with the United States Corps of Cadets (USCC) dietician. The cadet in my class said he never would have paid any attention to the vitamins if we had not talked about this topic and the wellness of subordinates. Mindfulness is a powerful thing!

Drinking at USMA was a problem, like it is at almost every college and university in the country. In DPE, we dedicated several lessons in the wellness course to the topic of binge drinking. The cadets always received a safety briefing prior to weekends and holidays, and guest speakers were brought in to address these issues across classes at different points in the year. The leadership at all levels at USMA and across all programs discussed and engaged cadets in this important conversation.

Following spring break one year, I received an e-mail from a cadet I had recently taught. Here is what he wrote:

"Ma'am,

I just wanted to let you know that your class (wellness) did have an impact on my this (sic) Spring Break. While I was home, I spent the night with some friends at their college about an hour and a half away from my house. Well, the first night I was there, I had some family trouble I thought I needed to go home.

---

[47] Cadets conduct inspections to make sure the rooms are neat and set up according to the standard operating procedures.

However, after thinking about it I realized that it was not a good idea to travel home. I had had a few drinks, and it was very late. I was not even close to being drunk, but I had enough to slightly impair my judgment and driving ability. I came to the conclusion that it was in my best interest (and the interest of others traveling that night) that I not go home until the next morning. A year ago, I probably would not have made that decision. As much as people complain about some of the classes we have to attend, I must admit they do work. It very well could have saved my life or someone else's life that night. I just wanted to take a minute to say thank you. Have a great day, Ma'am."

~ Personal correspondence from a cadet
3 April 2002

Of course, I struggled for work/life balance, too. Very often it can be the children in our lives who can remind us that the way we behave is not quite right. My commute from my office at West Point was about ninety seconds or two minutes on a day with traffic. It wasn't very long at all, and sometimes I wished it were. There is a lot to be said for having some time after leaving work to decompress and process the day prior to arriving at home.

There were times when I could become very direct at home, and when I did, my daughter Jackie would salute me and say, "Yes, Ma'am."

On one evening when I walked into our home, I was still very wound up from work. Shortly after I walked in, I began asking a lot of questions.

"What's for dinner?"

"What is the status of the science project?"

"Do I have any papers to sign?"

"Where is your lacrosse gear?"

210

I went on and on. Jackie, who was in the second grade at the time, looked at me and with the innocence of a child said, "Mommy, remember when you are home you are *not* the Master of the Sword." I had no choice but to laugh. Wow, out of the mouths of babes! After that I tried to become more aware of how I was feeling before I left work. Some days I would take a longer, five-minute route home to decompress and prepare myself for effectively entering our home.

Wellness is an important part of each of our lives. As leaders, it is important to pay attention to the wellness of those who work for us, and more importantly, make sure we are not negatively impacting some areas of wellness for our subordinates. If you believe that wellness is important, you must also provide the resources, both time and financial, to enable employees to participate in programs. It does not do an employee any good if there is a state-of-the-art fitness facility available, but no time is allocated for utilizing the facilities as part of a wellness program.

How about you? How much attention are you paying to your own personal wellness? Is your life balanced, or are you all about work? Remember, it is important to walk the talk because you are being watched.

Key Takeaways Regarding Wellness

- Write your own wellness plan.
- Participate in wellness activities.
- Encourage your employees to write their own wellness plan.
- Bring in experts to talk about various aspects of wellness.
- Provide the resources for employees to engage in wellness at their workplace.

CHAPTER EIGHT

WRITING YOUR LEADERSHIP PHILOSOPHY

You have read the stories about my brothers, my sisters, my mom, and my dad, as well as my husband and my children. I've shared moments that have mattered in my life and growing up in the Army. Each of these people have touched my life, and each of those moments have shaped who I have become.

Now it is your turn. Sit down and think about those moments from your life, both big and little, that have had impact on your life and have shaped how you see yourself in the world.

THE BE

There is an interesting, provocative movie, *300*[48], released in 2007, that depicts the epic Battle of Thermopylae between the Spartans and Persians.

Three hundred Spartans lead by Leonidas, King of the Greek city-state of Sparta, were marching to war against the Persians. On

---

[48] Nunnari, G. (Producer), & Snyder, Z. (Director). (2007). 300 [Motion picture]. United States: Legendary Pictures.

their way to the battle, the Spartans encounter Daxos, an Arcadian, and his soldiers who are also traveling to battle the Persians. Both armies stop, and it is clear from the reaction of the Arcadian soldiers that they are shocked at the small number of Spartans, and they mumble as much in the background. The following conversation ensues between Leonidas and Daxos:

Leonidas: *"Daxos, what a pleasant surprise."*

Daxos: *"This morning is full of surprises Leonidas."*

A soldier in the background says, "We have been tricked. This isn't an army."

Daxos: *"We heard Sparta was on the warpath, and we are eager to join forces."*

Leonidas: *"If it is blood you seek, you are welcome to join us."*

Daxos: *"But you bring only this handful of soldiers against Xerxes? I see I was wrong to expect Sparta's commitment to at least match our own."*

Leonidas: *"Doesn't it?"*

Leonidas points to an Arcadian and says, "You there, what is your profession?"

The individual responds, "I'm a potter, sir."

To another he asks, "And you, Acadian, what is your profession?"

The response, "Sculptor sir."

Finally, to a third he asks, "And you?"

The third individual responds, "Blacksmith."

Leonidas then turns to his Spartans and yells, "Spartans, what is your profession?"

The Spartans shout in unison, "Ah…ooh, Ah…ooh, Ah…ooh!"

Leonidas, with a smirk on his face, says to Daxos, "You see old friend, I brought more soldiers than you."

The professional identity of the Arcadians was based on their daily occupation: potter, sculptor, and blacksmith. The professional identity of the Spartans was that of a warrior.

The Army's leadership model of *Be – Know – Do* encompasses what is expected of a leader. *Be* is one's professional identity. Much like the Spartans, the Army expects its soldiers to have a professional identity around being a soldier. *Know* is one's professional competency, and *Do* is one's professional example.

The chart below illustrates the attributes that center around character and presence that we ultimately look for in Army leaders.

BE

Attributes

CHARACTER	PRESENCE
Army Values	Military &
Empathy	Professional Bearing
Warrior/Service Ethos	Fitness
Discipline	Confidence
	Resilience

Adapted from Leadership Requirements Model ADP 6-2, Army Leadership, p. iii, August, 2012. Headquarters, Department of the Army, Washington, DC.

The Army is a values-based organization and has been since at least World War I. The current Army values were revised in the early

1990s. There was an educational component to the rolling out of the values.

As an Army, we were not simply to know the seven values, *Loyalty; Duty, Respect, Selfless Service, Honor, Integrity, and Personal Courage*, we were also expected to understand the Army values. Once we had demonstrated that we had a level of understanding, we were presented the Army values card with a space for our signature on the back. Additionally, the Army values are a part of the Army's evaluation system. On the front page of the report were each of the seven values listed and a block to check YES or NO.

Empathy is an important attribute for leaders to possess. I recall as a young officer when I was single and had no children. A soldier came into my office and asked if he could go with his wife to a doctor appointment – she was pregnant. As I sat there, I thought, *She's pregnant, not sick.* However, I did let him go. Fast forward a few years, and *I'm* pregnant. I reflected back to that day when my soldier asked about going with his wife to her appointment and wondered if that might have been the first time they would have heard the baby's heartbeat or possibly seen the baby in a scan.

Because I had never been pregnant, I was not empathetic. I truly didn't understand. There are times as leaders when we don't always understand why those we lead want to do something. My advice? Ask why. It's the first step in understanding and one of the key behaviors around building trust. I'm so glad I let him go to the appointment.

Another attribute of character is the Army's **Warrior Ethos**:

- *I will always place the mission first.*
- *I will never accept defeat.*
- *I will never quit.*
- *I will never leave a fallen comrade.*

No doubt some will look at the Warrior Ethos and wonder how it can possibly apply if you are not in the military. There is a book, *The Warrior Ethos*, written by Steven Pressfield. In the introduction, Pressfield writes about the relevance of the Warrior Ethos to all,

> *"The Warrior Ethos was written for our men and women in uniform, but its utility, I hope, will not be limited to the sphere of literal armed conflict. We all fight wars – in our work, within our families, and abroad in the wider world. Each of us struggles every day to define and defend our sense of purpose and integrity, to justify our existence on the planet and to understand, if only within our own hearts, who we are and what we believe in."*[49]

Discipline is another attribute that falls under character. This is the ability to control your behavior in everything you do. The discipline of living the Army values includes showing up on time, being ready for meetings, planning training, executing training, and doing everything throughout the day to a high standard of behavior.

In addition to character, presence is the other major theme of attributes under BE, which includes military and professional bearing, fitness, confidence and resilience.

Military and professional bearing is the way you carry yourself, presenting a commanding and professional image. **Fitness** is a core competency for a soldier. Soldiers must be physically fit to meet the physical, mental, and emotional situations they will encounter. Soldiers are not unlike elite athletes. They must train and eat to have the stamina to perform their daily duties and be ready for an emergency.

Confidence is the knowledge that one will be successful and portray said confidence. **Resilience** is the ability to bounce back

---

[49] Pressfield, S. (2001). <u>Warrior Ethos</u>. New York: Black Irish Entertainment, LLC.

from a stressful situation. Our military has been at war for almost two decades. There are soldiers who have repeatedly gone in and out of combat zones during that time frame. They need to be able to come home, reset, and get ready to return; this requires a great deal of resiliency.

Character + Presence = Professional Identity or the BE

In developing your leadership philosophy, do the hard work of taking that internal journey into yourself. Barry Posner, co-author of the well-known book, *The Leadership Challenge,*[50] made the following comments about that inner journey during a speech at the Academy of Management in August 2002:

"...leadership begins with something that grabs hold of you and won't let go. Where leaders must go to find what grabs hold of them and won't let go is within. They have to explore their inner territory. They have to take a journey into those places in their heart and soul where they hide their treasures and then let them out to play. They have to examine them on their own and then bring them out to the forefront. We take a few steps in this direction when we ask and answer for ourselves such questions as: What do I stand for? What do I believe in? What am I discontent about? What makes me weep and wail? What makes me jump for joy? What keeps me awake at night? What's grabbed hold and won't let go? Just what is it that I really care about?"

The answer to the question, 'What do I care about?' comes only when we're willing to take a journey through our inner territory. Discovering what we care about is like finding one's voice. This is something that every artist understands. Every artist knows as well that finding a voice is most definitely not a matter of technique. It's a matter of time and a matter of searching – soul searching.

---

[50] Kouzes, James M. & Posner, B.Z. (2002). The Leadership Challenge, 3rd edition, Jossey-Bass, San Francisco, CA.

It is time to begin your inner journey. What are your values?

SELECT YOUR VALUES

It's your turn to think about your professional identity, the BE, beginning with the selection of your core values. These are the values and attributes that shape you as a leader, the internal qualities you possess that influence your behavior when you are not thinking. This is the way you are at midnight when no one is watching. These are the drivers and standards of your behavior. On the following pages are a list of personal values and a list of social values. Read through these words and select the top ten that resonate most with you. They do not have to be in any specific order.

You can select all personal values, all social values, or a combination of both. You can also include values that are not listed on the following pages.

PERSONAL VALUES

Accomplishment	Give of Self	Prosperity
Accountability	Global view	Punctuality
Accuracy	Good will	Quality of work
Adventure	Goodness	Regularity
Beauty	Gratitude	Resourcefulness
Calm	Grit	Respect for others
Cleanliness	Hard work	Responsiveness
Collaboration	Harmony	Results-oriented
Commitment	Honesty	Rule of Law
Communication	Honor	Safety
Community	Independence	Satisfying others
Competence	Innovation	Security
Competition	Integrity	Self-reliance
Concern for others	Justice	Service (to others, society)
Continuous improvement	Knowledge	Simplicity
Cooperation	Leadership	Skill
Coordination	Loyalty	Speed
Creativity	Meaning	Stability
Customer satisfaction	Merit	Standardization
Decisiveness	Money	Status
Democracy	Openness	Strength
Discipline	Peace	Success
Discovery	Perfection	Systemization
Efficiency	Personal Growth	Teamwork
Equality	Pleasure	Timeliness
Excellence	Positive attitude	Tolerance
Fairness	Power	Tradition
Faith	Practicality	Tranquility
Family	Preservation	Trust
Freedom	Privacy	Truth
Friendship	Problem Solving	Unity
Fun	Progress	Variety

SOCIAL VALUES

Accomplishment	Duty	Human Rights	Ritual
Accountability	Education	Individuality	Rule of Law
Accuracy	Efficiency	Leadership	Sacrifice
Act on things	Empowerment of	Learning	Safety
Adventure	Individual	Loyalty	Security
Authority	Entertainment	Love	Self-Improvement
Behavior	Equal Opportunity	Knowledge	Self-Reliance
Benefits to All	Equality	Majority Rule	Self-Respect
Calm	Excellence	Merit	Seriousness
Challenge	Faith	Minority Rights	Service
Change	Fairness	Nutrition	Simplicity
Charity	Family	Neighborliness	Sincerity
Civic Duty	Fate	Openness	Skill
Civic Pride	Fitness	Orderliness	Solitude
Civil Rights	Flair	Organization	Speed
Collaboration	Flexibility	Participation	Spirituality
Commitment	Force	Patriotism	Stability
Common Purpose	Fraternity	Peace	Strength
Communication	Freedom	Perfection	Subtlety
Community	Free Will	Perseverance	Success
Compassion	Friendliness	Personal Growth	Timeliness
Competence	Friendship	Pleasure	Tolerance
Competition	Fun	Power	Tradition
Concern for Others	Generosity	Practicality	Tranquility
Conformity	Genius	Preservation	Truth
Consensus	Global View	Privacy	Trust
Consumer Rights	Goodness	Progress	Variety
Content Over Form	Government Power	Prosperity	Wealth
Continuous	Gratitude	Protection	Wisdom
Improvement	Happiness	Respect for Law	Women's Rights
Cooperation	Hard Work	Responsiveness	World Unity
Courage	Harmony	Respect for Others	
Creativity	Helpfulness	Responsibility	
Discipline	Honesty	Results-oriented	
Diversity	Honor	Right to Bear Arms	

My Values

1. _____

2. _____

3. _____

4. _____

5. _____

6. _____

7. _____

8. _____

9. _____

10. _____

DEFINE YOUR VALUES

Congratulations, you have thought about and written your values down. I have conducted this exercise with countless executives, and about 95% of them had never written their values down on paper. You've done it!

Now it's time to define the values you selected. What do the values mean to you? If you selected integrity, what does that mean to you? Define your values in a way so that those who work with you will understand what you mean. My advice is to take about thirty minutes, get something down on paper, and you can refine it later. Also, don't make this harder than it is – don't overthink this exercise.

Here is an example of the way I defined diversity in relation to my role as the Master of the Sword so it was contextually grounded:

Diversity – *we are all different, it is that difference that makes us unique and strong*

- We have a wonderfully diverse faculty in DPE; each individual brings their own unique talent, skills and ideas. Everyone is expected and encouraged to contribute. There are no rookies in DPE, first year faculty members yes, but no rookies.

- I value your opinion; I will listen and take suggestions into consideration when making a decision. However, once I make a decision, the debate is over.

As you can see, I gave a brief definition and then gave a further explanation using bullets describing my expectations for others and what I expect of myself.

Define Your Values

1. _____
   _____
   _____
   _____

2. _____
   _____
   _____
   _____

3. _____
   _____
   _____
   _____

4. _____
   _____
   _____
   _____

5. _____
   _____
   _____
   _____

6. _____
   _____
   _____
   _____

7. _____
   _____
   _____
   _____

8. _____
   _____
   _____
   _____

9. _____
   _____
   _____
   _____

10. _____
    _____
    _____
    _____

Leadership Philosophy Guidelines

There are a few recommendations to keep in mind as you finalize your leadership philosophy. Keep your leadership philosophy relatively short, one to two pages at the most. If it is too long, it will not be read.

Check for spelling and grammar errors. Let others who know you well read it to determine whether it will make sense to others, whether there is anything missing, and that it is realistic, sincere, and authentic. In other words, is it you?

When finalizing your leadership philosophy, print it on your company letterhead with your logo. Make it look professional.

The next step is to share your leadership philosophy. Gather those you lead, and present it to them. Answer any clarifying questions that are raised. Share your leadership philosophy with your boss. It is a wonderful document to refer to during an annual review. Additionally, if you are interviewing for a position, take your leadership philosophy with you; it may be the reason you stand out from the other applicants.

Finally, live your leadership philosophy!

Please indulge me in one last story. We had a regularly scheduled meeting in DPE, and for some reason, it was changed to another day of the week — a day I had agreed to read to Jackie's class. I began the meeting and said, "I've made a commitment to read to Jackie's class this morning, so I will be departing the meeting early."

The next day, one of my young officers came up to me and said, "Ma'am, I want to thank you."

I replied, "Thanks for what?"

He said, "Thanks for giving me permission to read to my daughter's class."

I said, "You didn't need my permission."

He responded with, "Ma'am, I thought I was too busy, but when you stood up there yesterday and said you were going to read to Jackie's class, I thought, if she's not too busy, then neither am I."

In this moment, I was demonstrating the tenet of care, and this officer noticed.

Once you share your leadership philosophy, people are going to watch to see if you live it. If you selected and then defined values that are truly authentic to the way you live, then living them will be easy.

CONCLUSION

So what? That was a question posed by a professor during the first class of my doctoral work at the University of Georgia. He went on to say that when it came time to defend our dissertations, we would have to answer the *so what* question. What difference would our dissertations make? How would they add to the body of literature? My *so what* follows.

Whenever my husband meets someone for the first time, he asks, "What is your story?" The response to this question is usually, "What do you mean?" He will then go on to say, "Everyone has a story. What's yours?"

I believe I am very fortunate to be part of the family I grew up in, to have the education I received, and to experience the unique opportunities I had in the Army and continue to have in my post-Army career. We live in a society where stories are no longer shared within the tribe and passed down from generation to generation. Ours is a society of quick sound bites, hashtags, selfies, and where every single moment is lived out loud on social media.

After my sister Birdie read a draft of this book for the first time, she called and said, "Mo, I had no idea." Quite honestly, one of the reasons I'm writing this book is for my grandchildren. At this point in time, there are no grandchildren and none on the way. So, yes, it is for my grandchildren who have yet to be born. I want them to know my story.

I started this book by writing about my childhood and sharing many stories about my family. No doubt some readers will wonder why I wrote about that time rather than simply jumping into the leadership philosophy section right away. As I began to think about writing this book, I knew I had to start during a point in my life when I was my younger, impressionable self. Hopefully you will agree that the information I have shared helps illustrate the actual laying of the foundation of the person, the leader, that I have grown into.

The moments that mattered throughout my childhood and adulthood were powerful and, in some cases, they truly altered my life's course. Obviously, there are many more than what you've read here, but I made certain to include those moments that I felt fit best with the purpose of this book, and which led up to my time spent as the Master of the Sword, when I could truly live my leadership philosophy.

I've included stories from my career in the Army, times when I reacted well, and times when I didn't. I have also included stories about my children, Jay and Jackie. This was done after a lot of thought and conversations with the kids; they both agreed it was okay. I believe it's important to share the good and the not so good. Life is messy.

The final part of the book helps you to understand the importance of a leadership philosophy. I took you through the process of selecting your values, defining those values, and ultimately developing your own leadership philosophy. I encourage you to spend time on the exercises I've provided. These exercises will help you discover what's most important to you as a leader and what kind of leader you want to be, while encouraging you to reflect back on the moments that mattered in your own life and how they impacted you.

A bit of advice when writing your leadership philosophy is to not overthink it. Begin by just getting something down on paper. It might take you some time to get to your final version, but if you stick with it, you will get there.

You'll find in the Appendices that I've included examples of leadership philosophies from friends and colleagues. Over the years, I have conducted workshops with countless executives from all types of business and industry, and several have allowed me to include their leadership philosophies in this book so as to help you develop your own. You'll quickly notice that there are several different ways to craft your leadership philosophy.

I've included examples that are very brief as well as others that are longer, and still others that use acronyms or other interesting styles. I personally enjoy seeing others leadership philosophies and the unique and creative ways in which they are written and displayed. I hope you will enjoy this as well. Additionally, I hope that these sample leadership philosophies inspire you to craft a leadership philosophy that is unique and authentic.

In fact, I invite and encourage you to share your leadership philosophy with me, even before it's completed. I would also like you to share your moments that mattered that have helped chart the course and philosophy of your own life as a leader. You can email me at **BEtheStandard76@gmail.com,** and please include your contact information. I'd be honored to provide you with some feedback if you'd like on what you've developed.

Thank you so much for coming along for this journey, reading the moments that mattered, the big and little stories of my life. Now it is your turn to reflect on and discover the moments that have mattered in your life. Enjoy your journey of discovery. Make every moment count!

LEADERSHIP PHILOSOPHY EXAMPLES

JOE BASS, SENIOR VICE PRESIDENT OF DEVELOPMENT, HILLWOOD

Joe Bass, SVP Development

Leadership Philosophy

The following is an outline of the leadership values that are important to me and help shape the decisions I make. I may not always absolutely live up to them but they represent the expectations I have set for myself and are the values that I respect in other leaders.

Integrity

- Integrity is a basic characteristic for our team; it is a prerequisite for all we do. It is a consistent connection between what we believe, what we say and what we do.
- Integrity is an alignment between our values and beliefs, our words and our actions, and is a measurement of our honesty and moral character. It does not imply the absence of failure. It means having the strength of character to learn from past mistakes and move toward continual improvement. Integrity means striving to do the right thing for the right reason.
- I believe that leaders with integrity don't waste energy blaming others but rather take ownership of the situation and all outcomes. They also make it a priority to keep their promises and communicate any changes to previously approved plans and schedules.
- Leaders with integrity exhibit a high degree of "transparency". They build trust by being open. They tell the truth without distorting the facts or manipulating people.

"If you tell the truth you don't have to remember anything." -Mark Twain

Work/life balance

- A poor work/life balance can have negative effects on each side of the scales. Today more than ever, the boundaries between work and life are blurred by technology. It is up to the individual to define those boundaries.
  - One may choose to leave work at work and keep home at home and create a hard boundary between the two.
  - Others may blur the boundaries and spend more time working at home as well as taking care of personal items at work.
  - Both are valid approaches; however it seems that more people are trending toward the latter.
- It becomes important to manage your time effectively, so that work and personal time are both rewarding.
- We also have to take care of ourselves, taking the time necessary to eat healthy, engage in daily physical activity, and get enough sleep.

"There is no such thing as work-life balance. There are work-life choices, and you make them, and they have consequences." - Jack Welch

Joe Bass, Senior Vice President of Development, Hillwood (continued)

Communication and Clarity

- I believe that a leader cannot over communicate. It is important to express verbally what our thoughts and visions are. We often take it for granted that everyone knows what we are thinking. Even though we may have placed a lot of thought into something does not mean that others understand our thoughts instinctively or that they can instantly come up to speed with a quick word.
- I will strive to use clear concise communication to describe what we need to accomplish and why. If our mission is not clear cut, which often times it may not be, I will communicate that as well.
- Our job as leaders is to make everyone on the team believe in the mission.
- I believe that lack of communication leads to lack of trust.
- Be clear about your own message. Then ask: Who am I communicating with? What do I need to say? Why is it important? Simplicity is the key.

  "It is not enough to write so that you can be understood; you must write so clearly that you cannot be misunderstood." - Ralph Waldo Emerson

Respect and Humility

- HIP's team chemistry is built on respect. I value your opinions. Please value the opinions of mine as well as those of other team members.
- Arrogance is a cancer that will threaten and eventually destroy team chemistry.
- It is absolutely essential to take ego out of discussions so that dialogue, however robust, may be non-threatening and productive.
- Every role we are asked to play is an opportunity to lead.

  "You don't lead by hitting people over the head – that's assault, not leadership." -Dwight D. Eisenhower

Knowledge and Innovation

- Each day we are presented with new problems that require innovative solutions. Many times we may gravitate to the first solution which may or may not be the best decision. It is critical to make the effort to analyze each potential alternative with the available resources and within the allotted timeframe in order to arrive at the best solution possible.
- Resources include our own knowledge, the team's best practices collected over the years, consultant's input, the competition's successes, and published data, just to name a few.
- Solution analysis will probably include a study of positive and negative benefits, financial implications, and collaboration with our peers at a minimum.
- Even best practices should be challenged from time to time. Just because "we've always done it this way" does not mean it's automatically relevant.
- Effective leaders are in a constant learning mode. They are always working to fill in their gaps, striving to learn and improve in all they do.

  "Never tell people how to do things. Tell them what to do and they will surprise you with their ingenuity." -George Patton

JOE BASS, SENIOR VICE PRESIDENT OF DEVELOPMENT, HILLWOOD (CONTINUED)

Consistency

- We should build a predictable, reliable road map for every aspect of our business:
    - Our customers...The way we interact with our customers, both internal and external should reflect a reliable pattern of leadership. This creates credibility and fosters trust.
    - Our product...in order to demonstrate reliability, there should be no sloppy variations in our product or service.
    - Our internal policies...All team members should know what is expected of us and how we will be treated. This fosters trust and loyalty.
    - Our procedures should be organized and standardized without unnecessary complexity. We can't standardize everything, but to the extent that we can, we build speed, efficiency and discipline and ultimately reduce frustration across the board.

"In any team sport, the best teams have consistency and chemistry." –Roger Staubach

Teamwork/ Collaboration

- Our business requires a framework of many team members with different disciplines. Historically this has created dividing lines between multiple versions of "us" and "them". Conflicts between owner and contractor, architect and contractor, landlord and tenant, partner and partner, lawyer and lawyer...just to name a few.
- Better solutions can be obtained by uniting individuals into a single team. When leaders take ownership, they realize the benefits of all team members, and they look for solutions based on the strength of the team rather than looking to blame someone based on some weakness of the team.
- Collaboration builds on the best ideas the team can generate and depends on the mutual respect of each other's thoughts and ideas.

"Before you are a leader, success is all about growing yourself. When you become a leader, success is all about growing others"." -Jack Welch

Responsiveness and Accessibility

- Good leaders are good time managers. They should be quick to respond to questions from the team. Even if we don't have an immediate answer, we should honestly respond accordingly but follow up with a legitimate response within an appropriate timeframe.
- I believe that people will follow leaders that they can see. Good leaders should be available and accessible to the team, always willing to stop, listen and share insight.

"The first responsibility of a leader is to define reality. The last is to say thank you. In between, the leader is a servant." - Max DePree

Jim Bolger
Pratt & Whitney
Senior Customer Fleet Director – China Region
Personal Leadership Philosophy

I will be someone that others can always trust. For those that I work for, they can trust that I will faithfully implement their intent. For those that work for me, they can trust that I will empower, encourage, motivate, and defend them.

I will treat all with dignity and respect.

I will expect your diligence and competence, you will have mine.

Family is extremely important to me. I will always hold your family important to me as well.

As a team, we will succeed together.

Jim Bolger

Jim Bolger

DIERDRE BRITTO, CONTINUOUS IMPROVEMENT AND TECHNICAL MANAGER

Deirdre Britto's Leadership Philosophy

Integrity:
- Do what is right, even when difficult or unpopular.

Respect:
- Treat others as you want to be treated, when it is easy AND when it is not easy.
- Different is not a reason to dismiss or ridicule.

Ownership:
- Bring your A game every time.
- Take every task across the finish line.
- Be the best you can be in the now.

BILL CARPENTER, CEO, RGRTA

myRTS.com

The Framework of My Personal Leadership Philosophy–Bill Carpenter

My personal leadership philosophy guides my thinking and my actions, 24/7 every day. It consists of the following elements:

My Values: My core values are *integrity, honesty, commitment and confidence.*
- Integrity means doing the right thing. When no one is looking. When critics are watching. Amongst friends who would not care. Setting a standard that exceeds what is required.
- Honesty means expressing the truth. Regardless of the consequences. Speak the truth or be silent.
- Commitment means I am all in. Count on me not to quit nor walk away. I am in it to the end.
- Confidence means I believe in what we are doing. I believe we will accomplish what we set out to accomplish.

My Way of Doing Things: I believe in:
- Collaborative goal setting, strategy/tactic development and time framework. Once established we will maintain focus on achieving what we agreed to.
- Delegating responsibility. I intend to provide the resources and training you need to achieve what is expected.
- Regular two-way communication on progress and gaps in progress.

My Operating Principles: I value:
- Community benefit: What we work toward and accomplish will improve our community
- Our employees: They will have opportunity for engaging, rewarding careers with compensation that supports their needs
- Long-term perspective: We are working to serve current and future generations of customers
- Candid conversations: As I expect you to be candid with me, I will be candid with you.
- Lifelong learning: I have always believed in lifelong learning and will continue on that journey.
- Family: Success with family is critical. I will attend to these responsibilities when necessary and provide you that same opportunity.

My Expectations: I expect:
- Preparation: Agendas and priorities are clear; assignments up to date; everyone is ready for our meetings.
- Accountability: I will be accountable to the team and expect to be held accountable for my commitments. I expect you hold the same standards of accountability.
- Integrity and Honesty: You can count on my words and behaviors. I will count on your words and behaviors.

My Commitment to You: I will make vital decisions for the organization. I will work hard so that you have a bright future. I will be there when you need me. I will always care. And I will be your leader, not your friend.

Here is my signature on this commitment:

Date Signed: Nov 12, 2018

Raúl Correa Leadership Philosophy

<u>**Trust**</u> – Fulfill your commitment and honor you word.
- Earn it with your actions

<u>**Punctuality**</u> – Show respect by being punctual.
- This is the first step of trust

<u>**Honesty**</u> – Do not lie, do not cheat and be straight forward.
- Be yourself

<u>**Gratitude**</u> – Be grateful of what others do for you.
- Mean it when you say it

<u>**Work Hard**</u> – Give your best every day.
- Your team will respect you
- I will listen to the team.
- I will pay attention to what is important to you.
- I will give credit for a job well done and take the blame when things don't go well.

JINGER DITTMER, DIRECTOR, PROCUREMENT

Leadership Philosophy
Jinger Dittmer
Director, Procurement – Materials and Services

Integrity
My words and actions should be synonymous, aligning with corporate and personal values. I will communicate with transparency and share information openly. I will maintain confidentiality when appropriate.

Trust and Respect
I plan to earn your trust and respect by being of good character, working smart and hard, listening attentively, being decisive, honest and true to my word, and never asking you to do something I would not do myself.

You can earn my trust and respect by being honest and of good character, making sound and timely decisions, owning up to your mistakes, clearly communicating your thoughts and ideas, meeting deadlines and achieving results.

Once a decision is made, I fully expect all debate to stop and for all decisions, directives and plans to be carried out with professionalism, urgency and enthusiasm.

Fairness
I will recognize everyone for their accomplishments with equal respect. Everyone's voice will be acknowledged and appreciated. I will listen with an open mind. I will not play favorites. I will not discriminate.

Jinger Dittmer, Director, Procurement (Continued)

I expect the team to be fair by taking turns, telling the truth, playing by the rules, not blaming others for your mistakes, thinking of how your actions will affect others and giving the company a full day's work for a full day's pay.

Resourceful
I will work with you to resolve problems. I will provide tools, educational opportunities and support for you to grow professionally.

I expect you to work toward objectives daily, keeping them in focus and plan for success. Be prepared with multiple solutions for every problem you voice.

IDALIA M. GARCÍA, VP & ARECIBO SITE DIRECTOR, AVARA PHARMACEUTICAL SERVICES

 *Idalia M. García Leadership Philosophy*

Leading the Avara Pharmaceutical Services Arecibo Site is a great opportunity to transform our site, from Big Pharma business model to a Service business model (Contract Manufacturing). To transform the business, we need to exceed customers, stakeholders and employees' expectations on Quality and Service. The following are my thoughts about how I lead this wonderful site. I hope you can feel free to hold me against these standards and how we can work together to as leaders during our transformation.

SERVICE – to share the best of me and add value to others.

Create an environment in which everyone is willing to share their unique talents/capabilities and do their best to contribute to a shared success. I am willing to share my shortcomings and learnings in good faith to demonstrate that I continue to learn and develop as a leader.

FAIRNESS, EQUITY, JUSTICE – Treat everyone as a unique and special individual.

I foster and show fairness, equity and justice with everyone in and outside the organization. We will develop business processes and systems that enable fairness, equity and justice. Data and facts will be used to demonstrate success.

SPIRITUALITY, SENSE OF PURPOSE, FAITH – Design and improve with optimism, a sense of purpose in creating a shared success for customers, stakeholders and employees.

Design and improve for "what can be done" vs "what cannot be done". The why is creating the shared success. Encourage people to define "the how" and how they can leverage their strengths in the process to achieve it. Encourage them to believe in themselves and those around them. Help them exceed their own expectations.

CITIZENSHIP AND TEAMWORK – *Collaboration that transcends*

Be able to lead but also to be led. What we create together will contribute to the development and growth of others. Successfully lead in a constantly changing environment. Ongoing improvement does not end when team members take different paths but continues to grow in a new team of leaders they participate. We all contribute in multiple teams at home (family), work and community.

Lisa Haight's Leadership Philosophy

Working for EMCOR Group provides a great opportunity to utilize and grow our skills and knowledge in an ever-changing, decentralized organization. We have a clear line of communication and opportunity to work alongside our senior management and are able to offer and adapt our benefit and compensation programs in order to enhance the success of the organization, while taking full advantage of each others' knowledge and skills. Following are my thoughts about leadership and the way in which I lead the department, and my expectations of you as an EMCOR employee and member of the department. These are of equal importance and are not in any particular order.

Competence and Knowledge

- It is critical for us to maintain and enhance our subject matter knowledge so that we are effective resources and are enabled with good judgment
- This is best enhanced by asking questions of a knowledgeable resource, by reading job-related information, and through development classes.
- Being competent doesn't translate into a continual demonstration of what we know each time we are given the opportunity; it is more effective to apply our knowledge to the specific situation at hand. Remember we have two ears and one mouth for a reason.
- It is OK to make a mistake as long as you try to learn something from it.

245

Collaboration and Team Work

- It is important that I be a positive role model, not only to my team but to all in the organization with whom I interact
- Collaboration and team work require flexibility in approach when it is beneficial to the project—playing the devil's advocate when necessary and listening to other points of view and approaches.
- We are always presented with challenges, which we need to view as opportunities for growth and improvement in our ability to perform our jobs with maximum effectiveness.

Accountability

- Each of us has our own unique set of responsibilities that we carry out on a daily basis. This includes being here (attendance), being present while here (keeping distractions and personal business to a minimum), and giving the most we can to our job while we are at work
- We are accountable to each other every day we are here and will pick up the slack for each other when it is required
- Being accountable to each other also means we are understanding of each other's personal situations and needs as they arise, and that we make accommodations for them

Decisiveness:

- We have to make decisions, but only when all the available facts, options and opinions are reviewed and discussed
- It is always important to bounce ideas off of others as appropriate before decisions are made

- Ultimately, when the decision rests with me, I will make it and live with the results, good or bad, acknowledging mistakes and learning from them, as well as being satisfied with successes

Respect for Others:

- Mutual respect is of utmost importance in all interactions. This requires tolerance of others' differences and approaches to various situations, and assuming that each person wants to do their best and succeed
- Self respect is part of mutual respect
- It is never acceptable to act in a hostile or derogatory manner with one another
- Our own character is defined by how we act and how we treat others--Gossiping is toxic and sniping behind someone's back is detrimental to the organization
- It is OK to correct someone's errors but it has to be done in a respectful and non-aggressive and non-judgmental manner
- It is important in our dealings with the field that we are respectful and patient. They are the main reason we are here. They do not have the time to specialize in the areas of our responsibility and need our guidance. This is not to say we need to accept errors continually, but that we deal with improving the rate of errors in a respectful, instructive and patient manner.

Honesty and Integrity:

- These traits are absolutely critical toward success as a leader/ team member/collaborator
- We must act with tact and openness, and always with discretion when it is required, so our character is not called into question, as that leads to a lack of trust.

REBECCA S. HALSTEAD, BRIGADIER GENERAL, U.S. ARMY, COMMANDING

DEPARTMENT OF THE ARMY
HQ, 3d Corps Support Command
APO AE 09096

SUBJECT: Daily Philosophy

1. The purpose of this memorandum is to SHARE my personal philosophy on life and leading. I believe the most effective way to care for people is to get to KNOW them. So, the focus of this written memo is to help you get to know me and have a better understanding of who I am and what is important in my life. Clearly, to be given the responsibility and the opportunity to lead Soldiers is at the top of the list; it is an honor and a privilege. First and foremost, I am very much like all of you: I'm a Soldier, a daughter, a granddaughter, a sister, and a friend. In these roles, it is very important to me that I am a person others can trust and depend upon. Two words describe how I try to live each day: *"STEADFAST LEADERSHIP."* As a leader, I will do everything within my power to ensure a positive climate and work environment where people come first and missions are always accomplished.

2. *"STEADFAST LEADERSHIP"* is what I demand from myself and I believe it is what we must allow each member within our organization the opportunity to demonstrate.
My goal is to live the *"STEADFAST Leadership"* principles I address below. In doing so, I hope my actions and my example, not my words, will motivate others to adopt some or part of these principles and values for their own lives. These principles over many years have helped shape my character. Simply defined, I believe one's true character is "who you are when no one else is watching."

4. "STEADFAST" is an acronym and stands for: Soldiers, Training, Excellence, Attitude, Discipline, Family (and Friends), Accountability, Selfless service, and Teamwork. Below are some expressions of what I mean by "STEADFAST" and a little more about myself:

    a. <u>Soldiers:</u> People are our most valuable resource. The ARMY is all about people, from service members to family members to our civilian partners, both US and German. I consider all service members to be Soldiers, regardless of rank. I am a Soldier. To be a Soldier one must be able to both serve others and lead. Each of us, at any given moment, could find ourselves as the senior ranking person on the ground. Therefore, each of us must always be prepared (technically, emotionally, physically, spiritually) to take charge when in charge. We must never forget each of us were all younger and more junior yesterday; remember this when developing subordinates and setting standards. Lead by example. Demand the same from yourself as you would others. "Coach, teach and mentor" must be our watchwords for caring for each other and our families. Soldiers take care of each other and treat each other with dignity and respect.

    b. <u>Training:</u> Everything we do is about training. Quality training is the ultimate display of genuinely caring for our soldiers and their families. I strongly believe in leader development and certification training at all levels. We must train as we fight! Training is maintaining! Maintaining our equipment, our records, our health, our family structure are essential to our readiness and our ability to deploy. We must plan, coordinate and conduct realistic, combined arms training. Training is an individual and a unit responsibility. Training is for ALL members of the organization, officer and enlisted and civilian. I strongly encourage creative and competitive training programs. Physical fitness training must be battle focused and challenging. We must push ourselves and set high, achievable goals, not just meet the minimum requirements.

    c. <u>Excellence:</u> Know and live by high standards, both personally and professionally. We represent the military and the United States 24 hours a day, 7 days a week. Our actions must always reflect that we are a values-based, people-focused, and mission oriented organization. We must all "Talk the Walk and Walk the Talk." We must make every effort to provide responsive, premier support to our customers; remember, we are customers of our own organization. We must treat others as we would want to be treated! Seize the initiative, go the extra distance, and be innovative in order to achieve the highest standard of excellence possible.

    d. <u>Attitude:</u> The one thing in life we can control is our attitude. Our attitudes reflect our true character and how much we care about trying to "make a difference" and "make it happen." Be proud of yourself, your unit, your

REBECCA S. HALSTEAD, BRIGADIER GENERAL, U.S. ARMY, COMMANDING
(CONTINUED)

organization, your Army, your country. When you see a problem, become part of the solution! "Be all you can be" but not at the expense of someone else. Know yourself, your strengths and weaknesses. Take time for self-development and reflection and education in order to turn weaknesses into strengths. Seek responsibility, not glory and power. Work diligently and selflessly to make the team successful and cohesive. Do not worry about who gets the credit. Maintain a positive perspective. Count your blessings and look at the cup as half full, not half-empty.

e. **Discipline:** When we exercise discipline in all aspects of our lives, we realize success. We are able to choose the harder right over the easier wrong, accept risk versus gambling, and we are able to push ourselves to limits we never thought possible. Strive to be physically, emotionally, and spiritually disciplined. Disciplined soldiers reach and exceed the goals they set for themselves. Discipline is the major difference between a good organization and a great one! The greatest compliment we can receive is that we are a disciplined organization! Discipline is the final line between a safe and unsafe act. **Safety** begins with each of us. Risk assessments must be conducted properly and at all levels. We must all have on our "pay attention eyes and ears" and always look for ways to improve safety. Nothing is more important than a soldier's life! Watch out for each other and enforce a buddy system, both on and off duty.

f. **Family and Friends:** Whether single, divorced or married, we all have family. I am the third of four children and was born and raised near Ithaca, New York. My parents are retired, they are my best friends. My two grandparents played a huge role in my upbringing, with one set living right behind us for 38 years. My grandmothers both died in the last 3 years, one at 100 and the other at 88, both had huge impacts on my life. I have 8 nieces and nephews, but have adopted many of my friends' children and enjoy the role of "Aunt and Great Aunt Becky." My parents are raising one of my nephews, Joey, and I play a large role in his life. Children are wonderful human beings who provide a unique, and sometimes surprising, perspective for us! It is very important for me to balance quality family time and work. I believe it is rewarding to get involved with the community, school activities, and the church. Volunteering is rewarding. Family Readiness Groups are really Unit Readiness Groups. Use your talents and participate in a positive way out of desire, not out of obligation.

g. **Accountability:** Accountability begins with each individual member on the team. It encompasses both personal and professional standards: from your CIF hand receipt, family care plans, finances, to your supply, maintenance, readiness, budget, administrative and time management responsibilities. Hold yourself accountable for your own actions and accountable for the care and keeping of those entrusted under the leadership position you hold.

h. **Service:** Our business is all about duty, honor, country. None of us joined the military to become famous or be heroes. We joined to selflessly support and defend the constitution of the United States. The oath we have taken should be our moral and motivating compass for service--selfless service--to others. I believe true **LEADERSHIP** is reflected in our ability to **SERVE** others first. We serve each other, our fellow units, our families, our Army and our country.

i. **Teamwork:** Together Everyone Achieves More. The Chain of Command is "The Team." I believe in the power of numbers and two are always better than one. I focus on leader teams: Commander/CSM; Commander/1SG; OIC/NCOIC; Platoon Leader/Platoon Sergeant, and so on. Each soldier is part of the chain of command and must clearly know who is in his or her chain of command. Communication and cooperation are critical to the effectiveness of the chain of command. Disagreement does not equal disrespect. I believe in quality counseling. Counseling is part of training and leader development and must be conducted by all leaders. Teamwork must extend horizontally across our organizations: soldiers helping soldiers of other units, families helping other families, units helping other units and military supporting our civilian community and activities. The Chain of Concern is also part of the team and I believe that family members provide a critical link to our success.

5. Bottomline, I enjoy life, I love people, I enjoy photography, I love to laugh and I love to work hard! I look forward to sharing this time in the 3rd COSCOM with each and every one of you, learning from each other and developing a solid, caring, enthusiastic and winning TEAM!

REBECCA S. HALSTEAD
BG, US Army, Commanding

Rebecca S. Halstead, Brigadier General, U.S. Army, Retired, Founder, STEADFAST Leadership

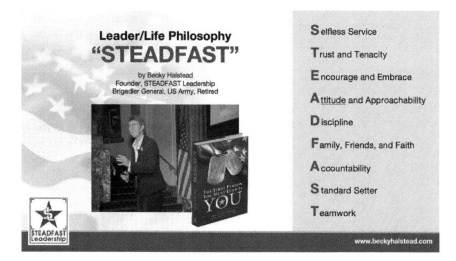

CAROLINE L. HARRIS, VICE PRESIDENT, TAX POLICY AND CHIEF TAX POLICY
COUNSEL, ECONOMIC POLICY DIVISION, CHAMBER OF COMMERCE OF THE
UNITED STATES OF AMERICA

CHAMBER OF COMMERCE
OF THE
UNITED STATES OF AMERICA

CAROLINE L. HARRIS
VICE PRESIDENT, TAX POLICY
AND CHIEF TAX POLICY COUNSEL
ECONOMIC POLICY DIVISION

1615 H STREET, N.W.
WASHINGTON, D.C. 20062-2000
202/463-5310

- Be kind. Follow the golden rule.

- Always be gracious. Be thankful for those around you and remember the higher you climb, the harder you fall. If you saw them on the way up, you'll likely see them on the way down.

- Be firm. Pick a position and stick to it. Endorse it and be willing to explain to others why you chose it, why it's the right path, and why you believe in it.

- Be understanding and forgiving. While sticking to your guns is important, never close your door to your staff or colleagues. Always be willing to hear someone out. But never be afraid to remind them why you made your choice and its right.

- Be open to change. The world is an ever changing place. Adapt or die. Always be willing to take a second look. At the same time, don't question yourself too much.

- Always remember the oxygen mask theory. There is a reason when you are on a plane they tell you to put your mask on first before helping children or the elderly. You can't be your best if you neglect you.

FRANCIS H. KEARNEY, III, COLONEL, U.S. ARMY, COMMANDING

DEPARTMENT OF THE ARMY
United States Army Southern European Task Force Headquarters, Infantry Brigade
Unit 31401, Box 88
APO AE 09630

AESE-B   10 March 1998

Memorandum For All Personnel Subject: Command Philosophy

1. TRAINING:

1. PT is the most critical task we execute, we can't fight if we are not fit.
2. Individual training and small unit battle drills and collective tasks are the cornerstone of training programs.
3. Live fire training is a must, it teaches synchronization and is a confidence builder; it must be safe and realistic.
4. Leader training and leader development is everyone's responsibility, we will have an integrated leader development plan, and it is our legacy to the Army and our units.
5. Risk assessment and management is a combat and training function, it saves lives and requires dedicated planning.
6. Maintenance is training and is a requirement for training.

2. CONSIDERATIONS FOR OTHERS:

1. We have only one type of creature in this organization: Soldiers, we will treat them with dignity and respect.
2. Diversity is a combat multiplier.
3. Harassment and negative leadership techniques are tools of the ignorant and indicate stupidity, cowardice, and lack of potential for future service.

3. DISCIPLINE:

1. Discipline is the heart of combat ready units. It is not the enemy of initiative.
2. Doing it right when no one is looking.
3. Good maintenance and PMCS are signs of a disciplined unit.

4. NCO's:

1. Officers don't have the right to do their jobs, and normally don't have the skills.
2. I trust the NCO corps, you should as well, I will hold them accountable for their responsibilities.Word did not find any entries for your table of contents.

5. FAMILIES:

1. Your families will be there when you are through with the Army. Remember that as you make decisions.

252

FRANCIS H. KEARNEY, III, COLONEL, U.S. ARMY, COMMANDING (CONTINUED)

2. I strongly support participation in family once-in-a-lifetime events. Graduations, births, deaths, and weddings. We must find a way to support our soldiers in their desire to attend.
3. The FSG is a command program; I will be involved as will every leader in this organization.

6. COMMUNICATION:

1. Doctrine: It is a COMMO tool – Know it.
2. Bad News: Doesn't get better, call me – I don't shoot the messenger.
3. Open, honest COMMO is the key to success.

7. COMPETITION:

1. You are competing against your potential and your ability to achieve unit goals.
2. You are not competing with each other or among units.
3. I will crush individuals and units who do not cooperate and share information. This includes cooperation with our higher and lateral sister unit HQs; we are not competing with them either. ONE TEAM!

8. FUN: I enjoy the Army and the people in it; you should too. We can be trained and ready and have fun.

FRANCIS H. KEARNEY, III
COL, IN
Commanding

FRANK H. KEARNEY, III, LIEUTENANT GENERAL, U.S. ARMY, RETIRED

My Leadership Philosophy is my handshake with you:

Health and Fitness are priority # 1.

Platinum Rule: "treat others the way they want to be treated."

Disciplined processes create agile organizations.

Trust your teammates and hold them accountable.

Developing leaders is leader business.

Open, honest communication is key to success.

Collaborate to achieve our common shared vision. Compete against our goals not against your peers.

Prioritize your family; they will be there when work is over. You cannot get back the time you miss with them.

Great culture feels like a family. We may fight with each other but if you fight one of us, you fight us all.

Maintain a life-long learning orientation.

So let's talk: "I don't know what I said till you tell me what you heard."

Frank Kearney

ED LAGOY, CUSTOMER SUPPORT, PRATT & WHITNEY

Ed Lagoy
Pratt & Whitney Customer Support
November 2018
Leadership Philosophy

Show respect and treat each other as you would expect to be treated, regardless of status, level or rank. Model this behavior in all aspects of your personal and professional life.

Listen first. Value input and ideas of others to encourage collaboration, alignment and the best possible solutions.

Encourage open and honest communication that provides an environment where everyone has a voice and is heard. Be transparent and expect the same from others.

Be the best you can be. Seek training and opportunities to enhance your personal and professional skills. Remain current, learn from others and encourage development.

Stay calm in the face of adversity, uncertainty or change.

Take care of yourself. Strive to achieve a work-life balance. Have fun.

MAUREEN K. LEBOEUF, COLONEL, MASTER OF THE SWORD

Set the standard
...Maintain the standard

Colonel Maureen K. LeBoeuf's Leadership Philosophy
Department of Physical Education
United States Military Academy at West Point
1997-2004

Teaching in the Department of Physical Education at the United States Military Academy is one of those great assignments in the Army. You have the tremendous opportunity to educate, train and lead the Army's future leaders. I want you to enjoy your tour with DPE. The following are my thoughts about leadership and the way in which I lead the department and, of course, my expectations of you as a member of this great faculty.

Care – *family, cadets, each other*

- Family – Your assignment in DPE will provide you with an opportunity like no other in the Army to truly spend quality time with your family. There are an unbelievable number of athletic, social, and cultural activities at the Military Academy, so take advantage of these varied events.

- Cadets - These are very special people and you will have lots of opportunities to work with them. You will teach several sections each day, have the opportunity to mentor, coach, and be an officer representative with a corps squad team or officer in charge of a club sport. A couple of years ago the Chaplain shared this word of caution if you have older children: *Don't ever let your children think they are competing with the cadets!* You can imagine this could really be disruptive in a family, so take heed.

- Staff & Faculty – DPE is a busy department, look out for and when necessary take care of each other. I often refer to DPE as a family and with any family; we celebrate each other's successes and offer emotional support when necessary.

Dignity & Respect – *treat everyone well*

- This is simple; treat cadets the way you want cadets to treat their soldiers when they are commissioned -- with dignity and respect.

- Treat everyone you encounter daily with dignity and respect; model this behavior.

Development – *personal and professional*

- Learning Organization - If DPE is to remain a leader in physical development, then we must and need to be a learning organization. Therefore, you must stay current in your field. As a physical educator you must read journals, attend and present at conferences, seminars and workshops. As soldiers you must also read your branch journals and stay up-to-date on the changes in the field, there will be many during your assignment at USMA.

- Learn what others do – There are several different offices within DPE. You must get around and understand how you interface with that particular office. If you understand what others do, it just may make your job and theirs a bit easier.

- Visit Army Units – It is important for the civilians to get to active duty army installations to see our graduates in action and to talk to commanders about their perception of our graduates. For the Army officers, going out to Army units in the second or third year will provide a great opportunity to re-green.

Managing Change – *stay ahead of it or it will overtake us*

- Arvin Cadet Physical Development Center – The demolition/renovation of Arvin CPDC (note we do not call it a gym) is in its third year. This is an exciting time, but also very challenging. You will be kept informed as the renovation progresses.

MAUREEN K. LeBOEUF, COLONEL, MASTER OF THE SWORD (CONTINUED)

- The curriculum is evolving, it changes somewhat each year. Last year we added two new courses, Aquatics Foundations PE 109 and an upper-class elective Level I Combatives Instructor Certification Course PE 413. Military Movement (formerly known as Gymnastics) has been totally revised. You must be aware of all changes so that you can discuss and advise cadets.

- In any organization change is inevitable, so it is important to remain flexible. It is also extremely important that you be supportive of changes that are implemented.

Diversity – *we are all different, it is that difference that makes us unique and strong*

- We have a wonderfully diverse faculty in DPE; each individual brings their own unique talent, skills and ideas. Everyone is expected and encouraged to contribute. There are no rookies in DPE, first year faculty member's yes, but no rookies.

- I value your opinion; I will listen and take suggestions into consideration when making a decision. However, once I make a decision the debate is over.

Pride – *in everything you do*

- How you look - Make sure you are in great physical condition and your uniforms fit, are clean, not faded, torn or frayed and are without wrinkles. The DPE uniform is unique here at USMA; therefore you definitely stand out and are noticed.

- How you act - Be the consummate professional in your deeds and actions.

- How you teach - Always be prepared when you walk into the classroom. Take time before and after each class to reflect on the lesson. I expect you to provide cadets with the very best instruction possible; they deserve nothing less. Seek out feedback from your fellow instructors.

- In your work environment - Keep it picked up and clean. Cadets are in our offices daily, set the right example.

- Arvin Cadet Physical Development Center - Our building is being renovated and we are currently living in the Lost 50s, but also teach in several other buildings. As I walk around our areas and USMA I constantly pick up trash. If you see trash, pick it up. If there is an area that needs attention, let the folks in FOPS know. Remember, USMA is truly one of America's treasures and we are charged with making sure it is cared for and well maintained.

Maintain a Sense of Humor – *you can't be serious all the time*

- At times we all tend to take things too seriously, it is important to laugh.

Wellness – *physical, spiritual, social, emotional*

- Develop your own wellness plan.
- Take care of yourself physically; make the time in your schedule to workout daily.
- Continue to develop spiritually during your time here at USMA.
- Make new friends, become reacquainted with old friends, and enjoy the company of your DPE colleagues.
- Stressed? Take a deep breath and look around, the United States Military Academy is a national treasure and you are a part of it.

MAUREEN K. LEBOEUF, BRIGADIER GENERAL, U.S. ARMY, RETIRED

Maureen K. LeBoeuf's
Philosophy for Living and Leading

BE authentic

BE caring

BE grateful

BE generous

BE prayerful

BE fit

BE flexible

BE kind

BE disciplined

BE empathetic

BE witty

BE present

BE fun

BE the standard!

258

CINDY MARKS

Leadership Philosophy
Cindy Marks

Accomplishment/Success
- Every role is key to our success
- Every individual needs to be engaged, work hard, and perform to the best of their abilities every day
- Active participation is expected
- Prioritize according to the plant goals, stay 'on path' and aligned with the Team
- Complete tasks on time and communicate changes/status often
- Communicate priorities to your employees
- Help out when you see a need

Accountability
- Communicate frequently with your employees and set clear expectations
- Hold yourself, and your employees accountable to the Team
- Set the pace
- Everyone is accountable for their attitude – be positive!
- Demand 100% of yourself and your employees
- Have the discipline to discuss issues so they do not become the new, lower standard

Competence
- Know your strengths and weaknesses
- Personal growth - self reflect to focus on your strengths and improve your weaknesses
- Continued learning to stay current in your field
- Be all you can be, every day
- Make the best decisions you can with the information available at the time

Cleanliness/Orderliness
- Set the right example to employees and customers
- Focus on visual management for improved efficiency and professionalism in all areas
- Have the discipline to correct issues as they come up so as not to set a new, lower standard

Continuous Improvement
- Never accept status quo
- Challenge yourself and others every day to improve knowledge and performance
- Embrace and drive change
- Open discussion for the benefit of the team

Integrity
- Work with integrity in all you do
- Be authentic, honest and open
- Set the standard
- Do the right thing, not the easy thing
- Demand the same of yourself as you do from others
- Admit mistakes and deal with difficult situations
- Build trust with your Team

Family
- Have empathy for personal issues
- Have respect for family responsibilities

James A. "Spider" Marks, Major General, Commanding General, United States Army Intelligence Center of Excellence

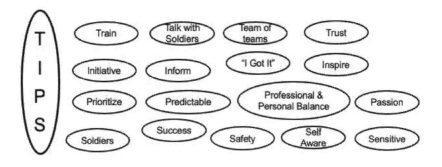

ROBIN MURPHY, PRODUCT DIRECTOR – FRESH FOODS, 7-ELEVEN

Robin Murphy's Leader Business Philosophy

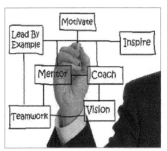

Trust
is the foundation I will provide and expect in return

Confidence
is what I will instill through my actions and support

Development
is what I promise, to foster growth and advancement

Feedback
is what I will provide always, as a means to improve performance

Perseverance and Integrity
to stay the course and always do the right thing

Act Fast, Act Smart, Never Quit, Improve Each Day

ERIC NUSS, BUSINESS DEVELOPMENT, NORTH AMERICAN DENTAL GROUP

North American Dental Group
Business Development/ Joint Ventures/ IDEA b
Eric Nuss's Leadership Philosophy

Change in the dental industry can legitimately be labeled the "wild west," arguably an exciting time for entrepreneurship from founders and leaders in this business to shape the industry and our market like we've never been able to. Below are my non-negotiable beliefs about leadership, the way in which I lead and my expectations of my constituents using my values and some of my favorite *quotes* from notable leaders and experts in the field of leadership as a guide.

"If you want to build a ship, don't drum up the men to gather wood, divide the work, and give orders. Instead, teach them to yearn for the vast and endless sea." — **Antoine de Saint-Exupéry**

My objective is to create a team with a common vision. I don't bark commands. My job is to convey "what and why" with passion that we are together and acting as one. It is not my intent to dictate "how" we realize that vision; that belongs to you.

"The function of leadership is to produce more leaders, not more follower" — **Ralph Nader**

As a leader, my ultimate purpose is to provide the resources so that others can grow. We are all leaders. With the right tools and resources people can do more than they ever thought possible impacting more lives than they connect with directly, whether they believe they are leaders or not. My expectation is that we are stewards of a vital role in our society- to develop leadership skills in others bringing out their best. Leadership isn't just something that sits with me- but must filter throughout the organization as a part of the company culture in the way we act, respond and grow over time. A key element of a leader is an inherent desire to be humble and keep learning.

"The single biggest way to impact an organization is to focus on leadership development. There is almost no limit to the potential of an organization that recruits good people, raises them up as leaders and continually develops them." — **John Maxwell**

Our world is all about people and relationships. I will invest in both. Headcount is a dirty word that dehumanizes the personnel of our organization. We need people to do specific work tailored to their unique abilities. Heads are fine when we are counting how many people will fit in a room, or at a table, but otherwise we deal in human count and talent management. I recognize you brought your talent here by choice and can depart by choice. My obligation is that you will never consider it! Lastly, all humans need fun in their life. 1/3 or more of their life is tied up with us at work, therefore the experiences we provide must not only make work more enjoyable, but we must also go out of our way to provide experiences that are enriching and rewarding away from the traditional work day. It's important to take our work seriously, but not ourselves.

"The art of communication is the language of leadership" — **James Humes**

I want to transform our industry and will model my behavior to align with my vision. I cannot do it alone. I will ensure your views are considered and will involve you in decision-making. I want you to feel a sense of ownership in the outcomes of a given project or the company at large. Communications and transparency are key. I expect transparency in the form of "Brief Backs" and "After Action Reviews" (I will explain and describe) to all engagements. All our gatherings must reflect our gratitude…."I'm am glad to be here…."

North American Dental Group • 11 South Mill Street Suite 200 • New Castle, PA 16101
Phone: 724.698.2500 • Fax: 724.652.9809 • NADentalGroup.com

ERIC NUSS, BUSINESS DEVELOPMENT, NORTH AMERICAN DENTAL GROUP (CONTINUED)

"Burn the Ships" — **Hernán Cortés**

There are two major types of decisions- Type 1 decisions and type 2 decisions. Type 1 decisions are irreversible turning points that require top executive leadership involvement. Type 2 decisions can be reversed if a business gets it wrong. Type 2 decisions should be made quickly by small groups or individuals (see above). As our business grows we must resist making everything a Type 1 decision. The result is risk aversion and stagnation. I will foster an adaptive, contingency-focused mindset while remaining flexible in our P4s (processes, practices, policies and procedures).

I will not accept conventional wisdom at face value but will always be accountable for my actions and results. I expect the same of you. We will not accept a lower standard for any reason, however, we will always learn from our mistakes and adapt as a unit sharing how we remedy the problems. It's not enough what I did in the past, there is also the future. I need to be a beacon to help convert VUCA (Volatility, Uncertainty, Complexity, Ambiguity) into our VUCA (Vision, Understanding, Clarity, Agility).

"A leader is the one, who knows the way, goes the way and show the way" — **John Maxwell**

I obsess over customer and team member experience. We must work backward from that experience both internally and externally to engineer and upgrade our services. I care about the long-term viability and success of the organization I serve. My objective is to delight customers to earn their trust. This trust earns us more business opportunities in more arenas. The long-term view and the interests of our shareholders and customers must align.

Teams must remain small. We will follow the 2-pizza rule for meetings. If more than 2 pizzas are needed to feed the group, the group is too big (5-8 people are the max) This allows type 2 decisions to be made with speed capitalizing on the skills and experience of the team.

I lead with integrity, doing what I say I will do. When I know a commitment will be broken I will communicate it immediately to all affected. I will always bring a positive attitude and my best effort to every project reflecting consistency. I expect this to be emulated by my team.

"Don't find the fault, find the remedy" — **Henry Ford**

Success is a team sport. No business can run a company all by themselves. We will count on the honesty of our partners, internally and externally to be forthright with their observed strengths and weaknesses of us, our competitors and our constituents, not to point out flaws, but to creatively develop solutions to current and future obstacles. We must embrace uncertainty without compromising resources, integrity, people, trust.

North American Dental Group • 11 South Mill Street Suite 200 • New Castle, PA 16101
Phone: 724.698.2500 • Fax: 724.652.9809 • NADentalGroup.com

263

ROBERT E. PARKER, CEO AND FOUNDER, REPCON

   Plant Maintenance   •   Turnarounds   •   Industrial Construction

REPCON, INC. • 7501 UP RIVER RD. • P.O. BOX 9316 • CORPUS CHRISTI, TEXAS 78469 • (361) 289-6342 • FAX (361) 289-6389

R. E. Parker
Core Values and Leadership Tenets
(To Live and Work By)

1. Always Practice the Golden Rule

2. Be Humble and Remember Where You Came From

3. Show Respect for Everyone

4. Always Be Honest

5. Have the Highest Integrity in Every Dealing

6. Clearly Communicate Core Values and Expectations

7. Do the Right Thing for the Right Reason at the Right Time

8. Lead by Example

9. Always Do More Than Your Share

10. Defend the Free Enterprise System

11. Work Tirelessly to Save the Country from the Secular-Progressive Agenda

12. Always Remember the Repcon Motto - "We Do Things Right"

JEFF SMITHEY, VP SPINE DIVISION, ORTHOPEDIATRICS

Jeff Smithey Leadership Philosophy

My leadership style is as a coach, and I take this responsibility with pride and commitment. I believe it is my job to help grow and develop people by giving them the tools to do their job or responsibility at the best of their ability. I want people to enjoy every day knowing they have someone in their corner helping them meet their goals.

C- Committed to delivering results and development of people

O- Open Communication and Trust

A- Attitude is something you control, so be positive and open to feedback

C- Collaboration and constant communication

H- Helping others meet their goals

2850 Frontier Drive
Warsaw, Indiana 46582
www.orthopediatrics.com

TRAUMA & DEFORMITY | SPINE | SPORTS MEDICINE

TOLL-FREE 877.268.6339
PHONE 574.268.6379
FAX 574.269.3692

DEAN TAYLOR, PROFESSOR IN ORTHOPAEDIC SURGERY, DUKE ORTHOPAEDIC SURGERY, DUKE UNIVERSITY SCHOOL OF MEDICINE

Dean Taylor's Leadership Philosophy

We are all leaders – we all *influence other individuals or groups*. We are also all different in who we lead, how we lead and why we lead. What follows is what works for me – my personal leadership philosophy:

Love/Service

Love and service to others strongly guide how I lead.

Love in this context is allocating to others my energy, talents and resources. Love and service are intricately linked.

Allocating to others, prioritizing their *needs* over our own *desires*, is true selfless service.

Faith

What I believe in, especially that which cannot be seen or proven, determines how I lead.

I respect each individual's right to their beliefs if they are also tolerant and accepting of others.

My faith allows me to comprehend better the incomprehensible.

Family

Family relationships are powerful and greatly influence how I lead.

I respect other's commitments to their families.

I love my family, and I am committed to giving freely and unconditionally to my family's needs.

Integrity/Duty

Integrity is integral to how I lead.

Integrity and duty are synonyms - do the right thing at the right time for the right reasons, even when no one is watching.

Integrity includes, but is not limited to, honesty.

Justice/Courtesy/Respect

Leading with justice, courtesy and respect create a highly effective collaborative culture, and is essential to how I lead.

Universal courtesy, which is respecting others, would lead to a more just world.

Aspire to the Platinum Rule: Treat others the way they want to be treated.

Excellence

Excellence is critical to how I lead. Excellence and optimism create trust and belief.

Excellence is the goal. Excellence is not a competency. Pay attention to details – they lead to excellence.

Strive for excellence in all things – who you are, what you know, and what you do.

Adventure/Innovation/Taking Risks

I am a better leader by seeking out and being open to adventure.

Adventure involves new ideas, relationships and environments, in line with one's passions, and associated with risk.

I am open to opportunities - especially those that are "outside the box." The resulting experiences create a rich life.

Passion-Fun-Joy

I lead with passion. Passion brings people together.

Through passion comes a remarkable capacity for work.

Make work fun. Celebrate with others. Look for joy!

Leadership

Leadership is about actions and behaviors, not positions and titles.

I am passionate about initiatives that teach the skills for effective, ethical leadership in health and healthcare.

I believe in the Duke Healthcare Leadership Model; it conveys a framework for learning and understanding leadership.

MALLORY TRUSTY, VP OF OP EXPERIENCE, ORTHOPEDIATRICS

Mallory Trusty's Leadership Philosophy

Learning & Development

It's important to maintain a thirst for knowledge, both personally and professionally. I will work to stay current in my field – reading journals, attending and presenting at conferences, seminars and workshops, and trainings to be able to provide good HR guidance to our organization. I encourage and expect others to do the same by leveraging our internal resources and soliciting outside sources. Let's Get Better: Together, we should strive to be better, faster and smarter than we were yesterday.

Fairness/Equity

People often mistake equity for equality. Equality means everyone gets exactly the same outcome - without regard to individual differences. Equity means everyone gets the same quality of outcome - something that fits their individual needs. I treat all our employees with fairness, and equity in administering policies and procedures, and encourage others to do the same. That doesn't always mean "the same" – but it will always mean "fair".

Quality/High Standards

As we move forward as an organization, it is important to balance our relationship-based culture with a more performance driven culture. I am renewing my commitment to a higher standard of excellence and accountability, and I expect the same from my teammates. To support this people-focused, results-oriented high-performance culture, I will:

- Work with our business leaders to ensure clarity of business goals and strategies with specific connections to individual goals and objectives.
- Implement operating mechanisms to Increase individual accountability for performance and achieving business objectives.
- Provide management with tools to better align and significantly differentiate individual incentive rewards for individual performance.

Customer Service

Human Resources is a support function; I am committed to being responsive, timely and thorough and provide helpful and relevant information to our organization's leaders to best leverage our greatest asset – our people! I am committed to:

- Responding to (or acknowledge) all email/phone messages within 24 hours.
- Making information accessible to our employees.
- Doing these things with a style and demeanor that is positive, friendly and professional.

MALLORY TRUSTY, VP OF OP EXPERIENCE, ORTHOPEDIATRICS (CONTINUED)

Flexibility/Adaptability

In any organization change is inevitable, it is important to remain flexible. I am committed to being a good steward of organizational decisions – supporting and implementing positive changes set forth by the organization. I will do my best to accommodate changes and adjust my style, and sense of urgency to meet organizational priorities and customer demands.

Respect for Diversity

We are all unique and different; it is these differences that make our organization unique and strong! I am committed to respecting and valuing the similarities, differences, and full range of talents that all employees bring to the workplace. To demonstrate my respect for diversity, I will:

- *Promote a workplace environment which utilizes the talents and contributions of all employees for business success.*
- *Treat all employees, customers and guests with dignity and respect, and the way *they* want to be treated*
- *Eliminate aspects of culture, policies, or practices that are (or may be perceived as) impeding upon the full participation of all employees.*
- *Provide Diversity Learning so that all employees may appreciate the value of this initiative for the success of OP.*

Find the Joy

Wellness comes in many different forms; physical, spiritual, social and emotional. While this is a 'business' and there are expectations of professionalism, I will take the time to focus on building relationships, taking care of myself and those around me, making friends, and maintaining a sense of humor – it is important to me to always seek joy in my life!

KAREN TY, MANAGER, FINANCIAL PLANNING & ANALYSIS

Karen Ty's Leadership Philosophy

Bottom Line Up Front: It's a two way street – let's keep each other honest.

Respect

- Treat everyone the way you wish to be treated. It's the golden rule for a reason; set a positive tone with everyone you interact with.
- Remain thoughtful of others by placing yourself in their position—remain empathetic and understanding.
- Hear people out – actively listen to others and their opinions.

Integrity

- Uphold honesty and trust in all your actions.
- "Walk the talk" by maintaining integrity when no one is watching.
- Remain truthful and transparent by taking a note from the Cadet's Prayer at West Point: "...make us choose the harder right instead of the easier wrong."

Perfection Perseverance

- Everything can be improved upon – get comfortable with being uncomfortable.
- Don't let perfection be the enemy of progress.
- Maintain high standards for high-quality work. It's easy to become complacent; it takes hard work to continually improve.

Humility

- We are the sum of those around us – lift others up by helping and guiding them.
- Don't tell people what they can do for you; ask others what you can do for them.
- We don't know it all – remain humble enough to find the learning opportunity in everything we do.

Humor and Positivity

- Find the joy and purpose in our families, life, and work.
- Laugh at ourselves and laugh with others.
- Dig deep to exude positive energy in the face of difficult circumstances. We can't always control our situation, but we can control our reactions.

LEE VAN ARSDALE, COLONEL, U.S. ARMY, RETIRED

COL (ret.) LEE VAN ARSDALE: Thoughts on Leadership

The following thoughts on leadership are based on a lifetime of personal observation coupled with extensive reading on the topic.

Great leaders share the following traits to certain degrees, sometimes situational. Many of them overlap and complement each other.

The centerpiece trait that is never situational is integrity. Subordinates must have the certain knowledge that they can trust their leader to always do what's right by them and the organizational needs, particularly when that requires personal courage.

A great leader leads from the front, physically when required, but primarily by establishing an organizational climate that is legal, moral, and ethical. My personal style is to treat everyone the way I want to be treated, to remain calm in stressful times, and to maintain a sense of humor. These traits aren't universally shared, but the healthy organizational climate is.

Great leaders ensure their subordinates are kept well informed. Not all great leaders are great communicators, but they recognize the need for this skill and find ways to compensate to keep their subordinates informed to the proper degree.

All of the great leaders I've with whom I have worked and read about possessed great energy for the job at hand. This vitality permeates the entire organization; people can intuit when their leader enjoys the job, and is robust in its execution.

Finally, a great leader is infused with a sense of selfless service. This is usually, but not always, combined with a good sense of balance between the professional and personal.

INDOOR OBSTACLE COURSE TEST (IOCT)

The IOCT test is designed to evaluate a cadet's muscular strength and endurance, agility, coordination, balance, anaerobic capacity, and the ability to make decisions quickly under pressure. A description of the IOCT obstacles/run follows:

1. The Start Line: Cadets must start from a standing position with one foot on the wood floor and the other foot on the end of a 40' wrestling mat.

2. The Tunnel Crawl (Obstacle #1): From the start line, the cadet must move forward 10' and drop down to a prone position. The cadet must move headfirst and face down in a modified low-crawl technique through a tunnel 20 'x 10 'x 18".

3. The Tire Run (Obstacle #2): From a running start, the cadet must step through an alternating series of eight tires such that some portion of the foot touches the floor inside each tire.

4. The Two-Hand Vault (Obstacle #3): With a running start, the cadet must simultaneously place two hands on top of a sideways

271

mounted, 4' high vaulting horse and vault over it. A right or left flank vault is the only authorized vault and the cadet must land on two feet under control, facing in the direction of movement. No hurdle, handspring or twisting vault is allowed. Women may touch other body parts on the vault such as the hips, legs, or knees, but may not twist.

5. The Shelf Mount (Obstacle #4): The cadet must mount a 12' x 3' wooden shelf suspended 7' from the ground. The cadet may only touch the wooden portion of the shelf. Use of the black metal supports and/or a back pullover technique is not allowed.

6. The Balance Walk on the Horizontal Bars (Obstacle #5): From the shelf, the cadet must climb over a 7' high railing onto a running track. The cadet must run approximately 35' and climb down to a succession of five, 6' long horizontal bars mounted 7' from the floor with vertical supports. After balance walking across the bars, the cadet must drop down to the floor and land under control.

7. Thru the Tire (Obstacle #6): From a running start, the cadet must grasp the top of a tire mounted 3' off the floor and jump feet first through its 18" opening. Diving through headfirst is unauthorized.

8. Balance Beam Traverse (Obstacle #7): The cadet must walk, jog or run the entire length of three successive balance beams. Each beam is 20' long. The beams are 13", 20" and 39" off the floor, respectively. Upon reaching the end of the last beam, the cadet must jump off and land under control on two feet, then execute either a side, forward or shoulder roll.

9. The Wall Scale (Obstacle #8): With a running start, the cadet must scale a 7' high wall constructed of plywood. The cadet must

land on two feet and may not use the vertical side supports for assistance.

10. The Horizontal Ladder (Obstacle #9): The cadet must negotiate a horizontal ladder consisting of 14 rungs spaced 15" apart. The cadet must jump and hang on the first rung and suspend his/her weight from each rung while moving to the opposite end.

11. The Rope Climb (Obstacle #10): Using any leg and hand method or hands only, the cadet must climb a 1.5" diameter cotton rope to a wooden shelf mounted 12' above the floor. The cadet must touch a red mark painted on the rope 4' above the shelf before touching any part of the shelf or the shelf supports. The cadet must continue the test by climbing from the shelf over a railing and onto the running track.

12. Two and Three-Quarters Laps Run on the Track (Obstacle #11): The cadet must pick up an 8 pound medicine ball and run with it for one lap around the track. The ball must be held with two hands in front of the body. The cadet must drop the ball where it was secured and pick up a baton. The baton must be carried for one lap in a visible manner. After depositing the baton, the cadet must run empty-handed to the finish line.

Reproduced from "Physical Program (White Book)" AY 07-08, pp. 28-29, United States Military Academy, West Point, NY

To see the IOCT run and the rules in action check out the video on YouTube: Rule of the Indoor Obstacle Course Test (IOCT)

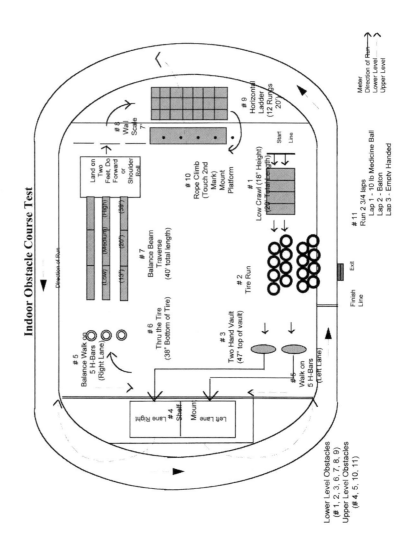

Diagram of the IOCT. Reproduced from "Physical Program (White Book)" AY 07-08, p. 30, United States Military Academy, West Point, NY

WELLNESS PLAN EXAMPLE

SPIRITUAL

- Give thanks each day through prayer
- Seize opportunities to help others less fortunate
- Serve as a spiritual leader for my wife and children
- Increase my knowledge and understanding of the Bible by weekly readings

PHYSICAL

- Earn the APFB
- Perform my back exercises every morning
- Develop and adhere to a regular work-out schedule that emphasizes all the components of health-related fitness
- Do not allow work-related activities to interfere with my work- out schedule
- Adhere to a well-balanced nutritional plan which includes meeting the recommended number of vegetable and fruit servings each day

- Maintain an annual physical examination with my family doctor
- Encourage my wife to be physically active and make time to work out with her

EMOTIONAL

- Continue to search for balance by emphasizing family time
- Use deep breathing techniques and imagery to promote relaxation
- Always try to keep things in perspective and focus on the "right" thing at the "right time"
- Learn to be less critical of myself and continue to improve self- talk
- Develop ways to unwind on the trip home so that I am not in the work mode when I arrive at the house

MENTAL

- Read current events articles and watch daily news to increase my understanding of global affairs
- Improve my business and financial knowledge by scheduling time each week to study our portfolio
- Increase my understanding of both TIAA and FERS in preparation for retirement
- Read articles, books, and attend seminars to increase my knowledge of military professionalism
- Designate weekly time to do research on basketball history so that I can continue in my quest to become a basketball historian

FAMILY/SOCIAL

- Spend one day each weekend with Linda and do not go into the office or spend that day doing work-related activities
- Communicate with my daughters a minimum of two times per week and improve my ability to listen to their needs
- Plan vacations and weekend day trips that promote family time
- Provide daily support and strength to Linda to help her with the rigors of her job
- Continue to prioritize weekend activities based on my family
- Designate one day a month to review my mother's financial statements and assist her with her planning

Made in the USA
Middletown, DE
08 May 2019